ROBERT MARTINEAU

# Waypoints

A Journey on Foot

**VINTAGE**

1 3 5 7 9 10 8 6 4 2

Vintage is part of the Penguin Random House group of companies whose addresses can be found at global.penguinrandomhouse.com

Penguin
Random House
UK

First published in Vintage in 2022
First published in hardback by Jonathan Cape in 2021

penguin.co.uk/vintage

A CIP catalogue record for this book is available from the British Library

ISBN 9781784709921

Printed and bound in Great Britain by Clays Ltd, Elcograf S.p.A.

The authorised representative in the EEA is Penguin Random House Ireland, Morrison Chambers, 32 Nassau Street, Dublin D02 YH68

Penguin Random House is committed to a sustainable future for our business, our readers and our planet. This book is made from Forest Stewardship Council® certified paper.

MIX
Paper from
responsible sources
FSC
www.fsc.org    FSC® C018179

# ROBERT MARTINEAU

Robert Martineau is co-founder of TRIBE, a nutrition company, and TRIBE Freedom Foundation, a charity fighting human trafficking. *Waypoints* is his first book. He lives in London.

# Contents

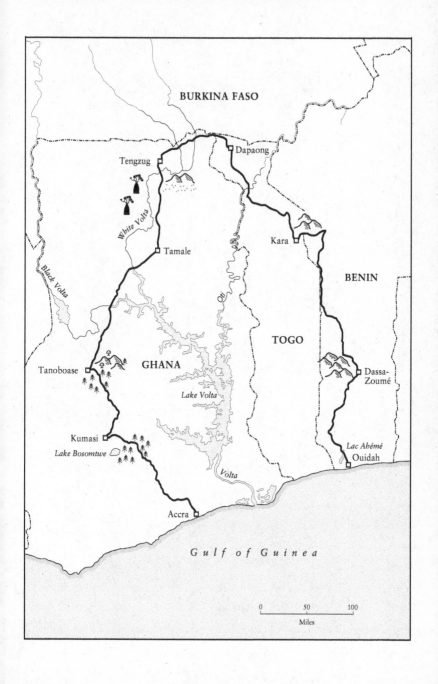

# Prologue

Most days that August, the August I started writing again, I went to the hospital. I watched the person I was visiting – someone I loved – slowly come back, day by day, to the person I knew. I watched, through the thin window of those visiting hours, a struggle I found hard to understand.

I'd come in the ambulance on the first day. Neither of us had slept the night before, him perhaps not for three or four days. Walking from the ward the first time, into the grey Acton light, I felt the adrenaline ebb away, then numbness: fear of the uncertainty ahead. Over the following month, that fear slowly faded: I grew somewhat familiar with the hospital; with the routines of ward life; the door-lock system and the sign-in protocols; the patients who smoked on the benches at the entrance; the community of visitors, nurses, and the policemen who each afternoon, it seemed, arrived to drop back a missing patient. I came, over that short period too, to begin to know some of the patients: the man with scars on his neck, who avoided eye contact and had a sharpness in his movements which unnerved the others; the older men, who had dishevelled hair and never changed from their pyjamas, who seemed to endlessly walk the corridors in search of a door that wasn't there; and the young men on the ward for the first time, who were adjusting to the new reality around them, like waking up in a new world.

Some days a volunteer accompanied one of the patients on a walk. I passed her once as I ran home from the hospital, under the bridge where a street of the grim, light industrial buildings that dominate that part of Park Royal meets the towpath of the Grand Union Canal. The first time I saw them return to the hospital from their walk, walking and smiling, I welled up. It struck me that what she was providing – a walk, company – might be as powerful as the lithium.

Part of me believed that already. I'd spent, four years earlier, six months walking in West Africa. I was twenty-seven then. I'd left my job and bought a flight to Accra. I walked a thousand miles from Accra, through Ghana, Togo and Benin, to Ouidah, on the Beninese coast. I'd been unhappy before I left, and I saw the walk as a way to fill a void. I imagined walking for months would clear out habits and feelings that weighed me down. I hoped it would work like a fast. I hoped it would bring closure to things long unresolved.

Starting out, the road was a shock. I wasn't prepared for the weight of my pack, for the humidity, for what it would be like to walk for ten, twelve, sometimes sixteen hours a day. During the first days, walking in the forests north of Accra, my body seemed to break down. I sweated so much my eyes stung and my face went white with salt. I threw up every few hours. I remember feeling I'd made a terrible mistake, that I wouldn't make it. Gradually my body adapted. It took longer for my mind: to get used to being alone for such long stretches; to being outside all of the time; to having nothing to do but walk, nowhere to go but the path ahead.

I'd started writing during those first days walking: each night when I came off the road, I sat in the guest house yard or at the end of my tent, writing by the light from my headtorch. Each month I posted a notebook home. When I got back, there was a small pile of them on my bed. For a while after, I tried to build a story from those notebooks. But I couldn't find a way to communicate what I wanted. I gave up. Besides, the world didn't need another adventure story by a white guy in Africa. At least, that's how I saw it.

Visiting the hospital that August, I started to think again about my walk. I'd gone away with ideas of wilderness, forest life, walking as meditation, dreams taken from worn copies of Thoreau and John Muir. I saw the walk as an antidote to things that were wrong in my life: too much time at my desk, staring at screens, partying, no direction. And I saw it as a chance to recreate myself: to become, on those trails, a person striking out on their own, finding self-sufficiency, strength, something purposeful. It's only with time, since I've come back, that I came to see those things weren't really what it was about. There were deeper issues for me to confront.

When I returned to my notebooks, after four years, I saw how much my perspective had changed. Starting out on the road, I was so focused on making the ground, on my own battle, that I didn't process the ideas shared through the places and people I was passing. I didn't dwell on the ways I was tied to the histories of those countries – the places once known as the Gold and Slave Coasts – through lines of conquest, slavery and exploitation that bound my home to theirs. I didn't recognise the extent to which I'd only got through because of the people who helped me along the way: how it wasn't a solo battle against the road, as I'd sometimes seen it, but a long chain of people, passing me from place to place over those miles, sometimes physically picking me up from the road after I'd blacked out. And it was only with time that I came to see how fully the ideas which were rooted in the religions and folklore of the peoples I walked among – conceptions of community, healing, ancestors, nature – had changed how I see the world.

Walking into the intensive care ward of a psychiatric hospital can be a shattering experience. It jolted me, violently, and that jolt made me think again about the road I'd taken in West Africa: how the walk had changed me; what walking had brought me in terms of mental freedom, learning to struggle, building connections with the natural world and the past. I went back to my notebooks and started to write again.

The following pages tell the story of the trail I took seven years ago: my experience of what it's like to go on a long walk, and the ways I believe a walking pilgrimage can help a person.

August 2020

# Forest

I

It's still dark as I turn from the house for the road. The streets are empty, except for the women in the yards, who light the first fires of the day. They pass hot coals along the row, moving the flame from house to house. I'm glad for the darkness. Walking with a twenty-five-pound pack and a stick, I must look strange. At this time, no one looks up.

I collected the stick last night from a carpenter in Kwashieman. The man made his trade carving ornamental masks for the tourist stalls outside the big hotels. He cut the stick from cese wood, which is dark like mahogany, he said, but light as pine to hold. He engraved it with symbols, each accompanied by a story: a sack of kola nuts to remind me to be kind; ram horns to give me strength; a great tree to keep me from harm. He treated the surface of the wood with oil to protect it from the wet, and moulded a thin sheet of lead to the base to prevent it splintering.

I didn't think then, as he first handed it to me, what it would be like to have the stick with me all of the time; how the tapping of the lead on tar, mud, dust and rock would be with me each day, sometimes from before dawn to long after dusk; how gradually, over weeks and months, it would wear away the skin from my palm, so that even years later, the flap of flesh between my thumb and index finger would be rough and calloused.

Then, as I walked the alley between the chapel and the petrol station, I held the stick awkwardly, wondering if I'd ever get used to it; aware too, suddenly, that there was nothing left to stop me setting out.

The stick is leaning by the door when I wake. My pack is beside it. I'd prepared sandwiches with sugar bread before I slept, which I'd wrapped tightly in film to keep away the ants. On the floor by the mattress, I'd left a toothbrush, a glass of purified water, two bananas and a candle. I eat one of the sandwiches in the candlelight, sitting up on the mattress, forcing the bread down with gulps of water.

My watch says twenty past five when I start walking. I take Malam Issah Street from the house, past the gas station, onto the larger Darkuman Road, which I follow through the city's northern districts. I'd tried to memorise my route out of the city: from Darkuman, through Lapaz, Achimota, Taifa, Ofankor. I repeat the place names under my breath, clinging, even now, to a sense that I know what's to come.

I lose the way. At each corner I ask for the Nsawam Road. I zigzag along a network of mud tracks, following the arms and nods of the old men who will sit on the corners till dusk. I walk this way for two hours, traversing the transition zone at the city's edge. The houses here are village houses, single-block bungalows with rusted roofs, country dwellings the city swallowed. The way the ditches are, the livestock, the mud alleys through which only scooters and donkeys can pass: all suggest somewhere remote. Yet, as the crow flies, parliament sits less than five miles away.

With the light, the tracks busy. Lines of women sit in plastic chairs on the verges. They cheer when I pass, as if

I'm a marathon runner. Some wash their children in laundry buckets. They dress the children for church in suits or patterned dresses. The children chase tyres with sticks and poke at bag-of-bones dogs. The dogs all look alike: skinny and hapless, with praying eyes. The little kiosk stores are called Biblical names: The Lord is My Shepherd Salon, Pray for Life Bar, Love Jesus General Store. Everywhere the paths are loud with voices.

I come abruptly to the Nsawam Road. Here, the vehicles are bumper to bumper. Horns rise from clouds of dust. I look at my watch: it's 8.30. Already I am behind. I try to pick up the pace, to force my legs to work harder. I measure my effort by the rhythm of my stick, which hits the ground every second step. I feel the added strain on my back, my breath shortening, sweat down my neck. I mustn't force it, I tell myself. I need to adapt to this pace; it's now the speed of my life.

2

A year earlier, on a Saturday in February, a day that was bleak and wet, the flat a mess and my head pounding from the night before, instead of switching on the television, as I usually did on those mornings, sometimes watching until it got dark outside, I opened a notebook. I wrote lists, filling page after page, in a kind of mania. It got dark. I kept writing, crossing out, scrawling, re-writing. The next morning, fresher, I took a clean pad. The ideas, jumbled before, had settled over night. I wrote a new list, in better writing than the night before, careful not to spoil the page with crossings out, as if writing this way would help the words become real.

No Internet, no electricity, no iPhone
Live outside
No more than forty possessions
One pair of shoes
No news
Walk for miles, every day
Only ever black coffee, water, beer
Cook by fire
Write each day
No motors
Forests, deserts, mountains
One rucksack

Then, I had a picture in my mind of how it would be. I'd walk into a wilderness, stronger than I was, a trail at my feet. I'd feel free.

Now, setting out a year later, it feels different. I walk on a stretch of mud between the tarmac and the stalls that face the highway. The road is busy. It's Sunday, but this is the main highway out of the city, and a stream of trucks head north. Children call out as I pass: *Obroni, obroni*, which means foreigner/white person. I try to focus on my steps, on the rhythm of the stick; to do what I can to shut out the noise. The truckers sound their horns. They call names from the windows: Moses, Gandalf, Tintin – where from, where to, how far?

The wind swells, drowning out the truckers. Dull, metallic clouds roll like waves. I try once more to pick up the pace, but I can't hold it. The stick has chafed my hand and the pack digs into my shoulders. My legs are shot.

The rain begins as I turn from the highway for Nsawam. I hope there's a guest house here, somewhere to be dry, to have my own space. I take the main thoroughfare towards a cluster of two-storey buildings. Most of the buildings here are single-room stores or homes, with whitewashed cement walls and rusted tin roofs. Some are painted with the logos of Coca-Cola, Airtel, Milo.

The rain falls heavily, in thick, warm drops. The track quickly turns to mud, and then, in minutes, to pools of red water. All around people are calling out: *Obroni,* where are you going? The storm has made everything frenetic. The women frying yam on the roadside rush for cover, holding sides of cardboard over their heads. People stand beneath the stalls to wonder at the sky. (In Ga, spoken here, rain and God are the same word.) Scooters burst through the dirt, chickens and gas canisters strapped to the backs. Children jog beside me, tugging at the straps of my pack. Some of them take hold of my hands. Because I'm not sure what else to do, I keep hold of their hands and walk on.

The rain is so thick I can see just a few metres ahead. I ask one of the children about somewhere to sleep. The boy leads me down a side path, then another, water swilling at our ankles. We come to a walled compound with a spiked metal gate. The boy bangs the gate. A few minutes later a man draws back the lock. The man wears a brown suit with a white shirt and a tie. He looks strangely formal in the mud yard in the rain.

It will be $2 to have a bed for an hour, the man says, $6 for the night.

We cross the yard. He opens a door and flicks the light to check it works. The room stays dark.

I crack my head on the frame as I enter the room. I can see, just. There's a grey mattress on a linoleum floor. Above it, a fan hangs static. Water streams though a gauze window, forming a pool beside the bed. I lie a while on the floor, running through the things I need to do before I can sleep. I lie this way for two hours, in a kind of paralysis, listening to the rain.

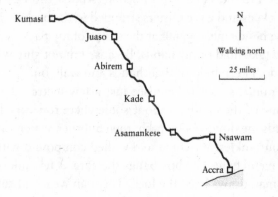

*To Kumasi, the Ashanti capital. North-west on forest tracks from the coast into the rainforest. Into the Ashanti region, west of Lake Bosomtwe, via the villages of Kade and Abirem, and the temple at Adako Jachie.*

3

The scrublands here, north of the lagoon, and far beyond the last of the old city dwellings, were once dotted with anthills. Local people saw the anthills as symbols of community, I read, and as gateways to the otherworld of the ancestors. Holding the earth mounds to be sacred, the residents constructed wooden fences around them. It was from those anthills that the city of Accra – which means *warrior ants* in the language of the Ashanti – took its name.

I thought of the anthills while, waiting on a visa for Togo, I wandered the independence monuments in Accra's main square: the statues of freedom fighters, the fountains, the policemen with white gloves: symbols of the new city. Across the Korle lagoon, the anthills came again to mind, as I stared at the children foraging among the waste of Agbogbloshie. Smoke from burning wires – set light to melt the plastic casing and free the precious metals within – mingled with the sea mist, so I could only see a short way from the bridge into the slums. Far into the distance, to where the horizon disappeared, slender figures wandered the smoking mounds of waste.

As I walked from the city, I imagined the anthills on the horizon. I pictured them as impossibly large, great working hives: gateways to the past and the forest. But I saw none on the road to Nwasam, and still there are none as I take the track into the forest. Whether I will pass them or not, I feel for the first time that I have crossed a boundary: that I've left the city behind, and the journey has begun.

\*

On the forest track, my stick taps only softly. Now the path is mud not tar, the softer surface absorbs the stick's pressure. The mud is copper red, with lots of standing water around. The mud is easier on my legs than the tarmac, as there is less force reverberating through my knees. The surface is varied: there are bits where the mud is churned up and deep, some where trees have fallen across the path, and others where the track is lost beneath water. It takes more concentration to navigate than the straight stretch beside the highway.

The light is also different in the forest. The big leaves at the tops of the trees keep direct sunlight out. The light filters through the gaps between the branches and the leaves, and the rays are continually shifting. There are no fumes, so the light is cleaner. The water droplets on the branches reflect the light back and forth like crystals. There is water everywhere: on the ground, running down the tree trunks, dripping from the leaves, and in streams and pools off the track. The air is humid. Moisture steams from the mud.

As I walk, I can see only a few metres ahead, except along the path which cuts thinly to the distance. When the path reaches a rise, the horizon opens up and the treetops are visible in every direction. I have a sensation in these moments that I am fully submerged, coming up from the leaves for air, like a diver from the sea.

I daydream for long periods. This is a habit I have from when I run. I sink into the dream slowly. I am still alert to the path, any people I pass, the sounds around me, but my mind is immersed in the story, as if I'm in two worlds at once.

The daydream starts in London after there's been a terrible disaster. The city is destroyed and there are only a few survivors. I am one of the few who made it. I am with a girl who also survived and we have to make a journey to build a life from nothing. Everything is down: phones, roads, power, government. We're not sure if our families are still alive, so we walk from London to Oxford, where we grew up, to find out. The roads are blocked with cars, as if someone flicked a switch and all the engines cut out at once. We see no one on the way. Our homes are empty.

The first phase of the dream is about surviving. We fill a backpack with food and bottled water. We find bicycles. We search for survivors. We wander for days, calling out for people, meeting no one. The most absorbing part is the rebuild. It becomes clear that the world isn't going to go back to the way it was, that we'll have to start over. We need to find a home, to learn how to live from the ground up. Over the weeks and months, we come across others. We settle a deserted village. We learn to grow food, to build. We go on expeditions to nearby settlements to gather fuel and books and medicines. A small community forms. I spend lots of the dream getting into the tasks I need to master: chopping the wood, making oil lamps, fixing the walls and roofs.

Over time we clear the debris around the village, the cars from the roads. The community grows. We have to find ways to preserve things, to transcribe what medical and farming knowledge is in the books and the minds of the people there. We have to teach the young. Sometimes we go on longer missions, to the far ends of the county in search of other communities or something we need. We get old there. The dream never ends exactly: I snap out of it when something distracts me, fall back in on another day at a different point, recreating other paths within it.

I never stop to think what the story means or why I get absorbed in that one over any other. But daydreaming as I walk works something like a drug. My sense of thoughts flowing through my mind heightens. Everything outside of myself and the trail through the trees fades out. I lose track of time. I feel I have enough energy to keep on forever.

4

Sometimes I lose the thread that binds my mind and feet. I've come fifty miles since yesterday morning, and I'm tiring. My stick hits the ground unevenly, my pack sags, and I stumble. Where before I could sense the terrain without looking, now, after many hours, my feet cannot smoothly navigate the bumps and sinks. The track rises and falls, on and on through the trees. I stub my toes on rocks and logs. I am not quite staggering, but I no longer move cleanly. I get the weight of my steps wrong, so that as I hit the ground, I come down heavily, and my ankles absorb pressure they were not built for. The blister on the heel of my left foot stabs with each misstep.

I try to remember why I am here, to take myself out of the heat and mud, back to the clean, dry air, the sterile brightness, of where I left behind.

I worked then on the sixth floor of a ten-storey office block overlooking Liverpool Street Station.

I often stayed late in the office, sometimes to the early hours of the morning. I try to picture the canteen. Only the junior lawyers ate there, a metallic hall with strip lighting and huge windows that looked out onto buildings whose lights never turned off. If we worked past 9 p.m., we were allowed to charge up to £6 of food to the client. This was enough for pasta salad or fish and chips, a piece of fruit, a drink and a chocolate bar. Often

I took the food to go, in a polystyrene box. The smell of the meal clung to the conditioned air. When I'd eaten, I was drowsy, so I'd drink a Coke to sharpen me and sit, back arched, before the screen, ready to push on into the night.

I was twenty-five when I started working at the law firm. Within a few months, as the newness wore off, I noticed myself change. The first thing was my eyes: each week, it seemed, my eyesight was worse. After a while, I could no longer read the signs across the railway concourse. Sores had come up on the back of my legs, too: eczema I hadn't had since I was a child. I'd put on weight: I could grab a roll of belly fat that hadn't been there before. Hunched at my desk, I could feel the roll above my belt.

Mentally, too, I was different. I'd sit for hours at my computer, but when I tried to think back to what I'd been doing, I couldn't track the time or the tasks. I checked my phone every few minutes: emails, Facebook, news, in a near-continuous cycle. I wasn't sleeping. Some mornings I woke so tired I felt hungover even when I hadn't drunk. Lots of the time I felt anxious, without knowing why or how to feel better.

The only way I knew to feel release was to run. At the law firm I got into the habit of running home a couple of nights a week. Often it was late when I ran, sometimes past midnight, and the streets were deserted. I ran along the river, past the lit-up bridges. I loved that time of night. When I'd made it home – about six miles – I felt clear, like I'd dived into cold water. The tiredness, the taste of the canteen, the anxiety, had gone away.

When I started to think about a pilgrimage, in part I was searching for that feeling.

5

Thick roots, stained grey with moss, spill from the mud in the forests north of Asamankese. The track narrows. Trees with wide, flat leaves and white flowers hang over the path. Dragonflies hover among the trees. I've walked for three days to this point. It's rained each day at this time, and now it begins again. The raindrops bounce like pellets from the leaves. I use my stick to keep steady in the mud. In places, pools submerge the path, and I wade through brown water.

I'd traced with a highlighter the tracks I intended to follow through the forest. But only the larger forest roads were on the map, and I don't always know if I'm on the right path. Each morning I write on my hand the names of the villages I'll pass along the way. When I reach a village, I ask the name of the next, to reassure me that I'm walking the right track. I've come eighty miles to this point. I'm heading now into the Ashanti region. The Ashanti capital, Kumasi, is four days' walk.

Beginning to think about this journey, I sat one Sunday in the basement room of a map store in Covent Garden, and took out maps from all over the world: the Highlands, Galicia, the Euphrates, Patagonia, the Appalachians, the Mountains of the Moon, the Jungfrau, Ethiopia, West Africa, the Himalayas. Some of the regions were famous pilgrimage routes, like the Way of St James or Kailash; others were places I'd read about somewhere or seen on nature shows. I covered a table with maps.

I'd first heard of the Bight of Benin – the stretch of West African coast between Ghana and Nigeria – two years earlier, in conversation with a traveller in Namibia. The man was a rig worker who worked half the year offshore on the Gulf of Guinea; the other half he came to land and spent what he earned. He described himself as Rhodesian, but travelled continuously, he said, never settling long enough to owe taxes.

On one journey, he'd travelled from the Ebrié Lagoon to Calabar, moving east from Côte d'Ivoire across Ghana, Togo, Benin and Nigeria. He spoke of masked dancers, extraordinary healing, trees that turned to snakes before his eyes. I wasn't sure what was real and what were mad ramblings, but I always remembered his stories. Benin was the last animist country in the world, he said.

Soon after, I read Ben Okri's book, *The Famished Road*. Azaro, the hero of that story, is caught between the spirit and living worlds: the room in his compound, where creditors beat the door and rats gnaw the floorboards, and the forests where the human world melts away. In that book, dreams, the past, politics, spirits, poverty, fairytales, slavery; all weaved through life in ways I hadn't imagined before.

I read more by Ben Okri, then other writers from or inspired by West Africa. This part of West Africa – the areas once known as the Gold and Slave Coasts – had experienced injustice on an unimaginable scale. But I came to think there would be ideas about life and memory there that might help me. For the same reason some people travel to Jerusalem or Kailash because of the stories they've heard, I was drawn to the Bight of Benin. And with all the naivety of a young Western man, I built the place up in my mind: the idea of it as remote, as a wild place, a place with hard roads and rough ways of life, somewhere there was old wisdom, somewhere I could test myself, a place capable of breaking me down, forcing me to build myself back up. However misguided that was, however little I knew of the roads I stared at on the map, or of the peoples who walked them, I came to the Bight of Benin with the same hope most people carry to places of pilgrimage: in search of resolution, of becoming whole.

Each morning I woke early to plan the route before work. I used maps and books, drawing crosses on the map to mark places I read about. Slowly I developed a route. I planned to start in Accra, Ghana's capital city, and to end at Ouidah, a former slave port on the coast of Benin, sacred to traditional local religions. The crosses I drew between the two places became my waypoints: a mix of shrines, forest outposts, mountains, monasteries, border crossings and the region's oldest cities.

Joining the points together, the route stretched in an arc of 1,100 miles, from Ghana's coast, north to the edge of the Sahel, and back south to the Atlantic. The route passed through three countries: Ghana, Togo and Benin, crossing tropical forest, desert savannah and mountains. Mostly I would follow small roads and mud tracks, like the ones I'm on now, marked with dashes on my map. In the more remote regions to the north, there were no roads linking the points on my map, but I hoped I'd find a trail.

These were the waypoints I marked on my map:

Mile 160. Kumasi, capital of the Ashanti Kingdom.

Mile 280. Tanoboase, a forest shrine. Sacred to the Ashanti and the Abron.

Mile 430. Tamale, the administrative centre of northern Ghana.

Mile 530. Tengzug, a hilltop shrine at the edge of the Sahel, northern Ghana. Sacred to the Tallensi.

Mile 640. Dapaong, the first town past the Ghana–Togo border.

Mile 760. Kara, the last town before the crossing to Benin.
Mile 970: Dassa-Zoumé, a hilltop shrine. Site of one of the
    largest pilgrimages in West Africa.
Mile 1,100: Ouidah.

Drawing the route, they were just places on the map. But even so soon after starting out, they've become more. I've begun to think in waypoints. Everything I do I consider in terms of how it moves me closer to the next. Right now, the only goal in my life is to make it to Kumasi.

6

In the winter of 1845 – several months after Henry Thoreau had first moved to the woods at Walden – the forest lay under a foot of snow. The lake, over thirty metres deep at its centre, froze at its fringes. Maple, white birch and spruce grew from the bank's marshy sands. Bear, bison and moose roamed the trees, in which fish hawks nested. Thoreau lived for two years there, in a cabin in a clearing, more or less shut off from the outside world.

'I went to the woods because I wanted to live deliberately,' Thoreau wrote. 'To front only the essential facts of life.'

His account of the experience – *Walden* – has become a type of bible for people searching ways to live minimally, in nature. When I first read *Walden*, in my final year at school, I thought of it as distant: a piece of old literature, like the books I studied in class. Re-reading *Walden* before I left, I read it differently: I saw Thoreau as someone who'd learnt from experience, making a simple point: *Spend more time in nature for your own good.*

But I wasn't sure what Thoreau meant by some of the things he wrote. I didn't know what living deliberately was. 'I did not wish to live what was not life,' he said. What did he mean?

He seemed to get closer to whatever it was at Walden. Partly, it was being exposed to the forest. In the woods, Thoreau pulled away the layers of life he didn't see value in, got closer to what he called wildness. But it was also the discipline of how he lived. Building the cabin was as important as being in it or what it allowed him to be near. The process of construction, log by log, was part of how he found what he was looking for.

I try to visualise my steps like Thoreau's logs: building up, one on top of the other, into something that can house a new life.

At this time, an hour before dusk, the bugs rise like mist. There are so many the air seems to thicken. They cling to the sweat on my arms and neck. I pour water over my head to try to wash them away. I light cigarettes to smoke them off. My whole body itches. I slip and slide in the mud, yelling at the mosquitoes, the thorns which tear at my arms, the webs that cling to my face.

Planning the journey, reading books like *Walden*, I pictured myself in the woods. I transcribed passages from Thoreau and John Muir. I had become estranged from the natural world, I thought, estranged from who I was. When people at home asked if I knew what I was doing, I shrugged it off. Wouldn't I get lonely and sick? they asked. How would I look after myself? It would be worth it to feel free, I thought. I wanted what Thoreau and Muir got from the forest, the feelings they wrote, the words they used.

Now I'm here, it's different. I want to be out of the mud and the bugs, away from the humid air and the weight of my pack. But I have nowhere to go. The only way out is to keep on to the next village or go back to the last. Both are hours' walk away. Perhaps I should go home, admit it was a mistake. The shame would be unbearable.

My stomach cramps. I stop to squat off the track. Nothing comes. I clasp my legs; let my head hang between my knees. Close up, the whole forest floor seems to move. Water trickles from the ferns, and from the red flowers which look like flames, and the half-sunk sides of bark, down to where the vegetation is mashed up and dying. By the roots of the trees, droplets form on the mushroom heads, which shudder, even though there is no breeze; no air at all, it feels to me. Sweat runs from my face, arms and thighs. Water, too, seems to be bubbling back from the earth, from the crushed wood, the remnants of the leaves. Thick-bodied red ants and small black ones carry flakes of vegetation into the ground. There are slugs, millipedes, globules of sap in the mud. Every few hours I've thrown up or shat in the trees. The cramps in my stomach come in waves. I try to eat, as if it were as simple as fuelling an engine. I move more and more slowly. I wonder if I'm ill or just adjusting. It makes little difference now. I need only to keep on, I tell myself, to reach the village by nightfall.

In Japan forest walking is prescribed like medicine. There, sixty woodland zones are registered as forest therapy sites within reach of downtown areas. Doctors advise city residents spend at least thirty minutes a week walking in the forest, to improve physical and mental health.

Doctors with a focus on forest walking, which they call *shinrin-yoku*, have run studies to try to understand its physiological impact. Something about the woods, they say, seems to calm people down. Walking among trees causes participants' pulse rates to lower and blood pressure to fall. Cortisol is lower in people's saliva when walking in a forest than in the city. Levels of parasympathetic activity, a part of the auto-nervous response system that engages when people feel relaxed and safe, rise when people walk in the woods.

I wonder what my cortisol is doing. There were no bugs, it seemed, in the *shinrin-yoku* forests, no stumbling in the mud.

A study from the 1980s found that just looking at trees can change the way our bodies work. In 1984 an architect, Roger Ulrich, ran an experiment to see whether having a forest view impacted patient recovery times. Ulrich analysed records of patients who had recovered from gall bladder surgery in a Pennsylvania hospital during the 1970s. One set of patients recuperated in rooms looking onto a wall; a second group had rooms with a view of trees. He found the patients who could see the trees recovered and were discharged from hospital on average a day faster than those in rooms that faced the wall.

A Korean team attempted to visualise the brain reacting to a forest scene like Ulrich's window view. When people looked at urban images, their scans showed heightened activity in the parts of the brain that recall emotional distress. Forest scenes triggered blood to brain areas associated with self-awareness and empathy.

Scientists can see the ways forests impact people's bodies and minds, but they don't understand why.

John Muir, who spent years walking alone in the forests of Yosemite in the late nineteenth century, thought it had something to do with secretions from trees. 'A tree does good like a medicine,' he wrote in a diary from Yosemite, 'enriching the air with resin and balsam'. As with many of Muir's ideas, which seemed to emerge almost out of instinct, something like this theory has since been taken up. Plants emit oils to defend against bacteria. *Shinrin-yoku* research suggests that exposure to these oils – phytoncides – is part of the reason people feel rejuvenated in the woods. For Muir it was also spiritual. The clearest way into the Universe, he said, is through a forest wilderness.

Our eyes seem adapted to look on forests. Richard Taylor, a physicist, proposed that the human eye is drawn to fractals, complex patterns that repeat at finer and finer magnification. Taylor began his work on Jackson Pollock paintings, suggesting that people stare because of the paintings' fractal patterns. Pollock's art, Taylor says, shares a patterned structure similar to a forest: the closer you look, the more you see.

Things in nature are often fractal. If you zoom in to a snowflake, a mountain range, a fern leaf, you see the same shape inside itself again and again. A forest is fractal, as the canopy, the individual trees, the leaves, the leaf fibres, down even to the the pigments in the chlorophyll, are repeating the same pattern over and over at different scales.

Participants in Taylor's research calmed when they stared at fractal images. Taylor's work indicates that fractal patterns have a sensory impact, and as flames or waves can be mesmerising, the visual repetition of trees, branches and leaves in the forest is soothing.

I reach Kade near dusk.

Kade is a small town at the intersection of two dirt roads in the Nsuensa Forest. On the road through town, there are bread, fruit and soft drink stands. Stallholders lay out bananas and yams on cloth beneath parasols. Beyond the ditches, there are kiosk bars and general stores.

The guest house is in a compound off a dirt track. There are a few trees in the yard, dogs beneath them. A girl with long hair and a scar above her eye sits on the porch shelling beans, while another girl braids her hair. The girl with braids – Beatrice – shows me to a room. She brings a bucket of warm water to wash with.

I wash for the first time in two days, using a plastic jug to pour water over my head. I rinse my clothes and hang them to dry. I treat my feet with iodine and dress the blisters as best I can. I lay out a pile of things for the morning, and pack the remaining items into my rucksack.

The forest looks closer in the dark. The trees, now in silhouette, and the creepers which hang from them, and the upper branches which rise to the sky, have spread, casting vast shadows on the mud yard floor. As the light fades, the vegetation seems to liven. The leaves sway, and I hear the brushing of the leaves above the generators which burn on the main strip. Moths circle the fire in the yard. In the low sky there are bats.

Beatrice and her sister prepare a meal by the fire. A pot, two knives and a pile of vegetables are laid on a cloth. We chop tomatoes, okra and chillies.

Beatrice says they are at the guesthouse to help their mother.

Where are my wife, my children? she asks.

Her sister – Blessing – starts to laugh. She is going to ask you to marry her and go to America!

Beatrice hits her with the cloth.

Her dream is to join the police, Beatrice says. She's dreamed of this since she was a child. But first she must help her mother here. When her mother is better, she will return to school to complete her training. At church she prays for her family, she says, that she will realise her dream to be a policewoman, that she will meet her husband and have a family of her own.

I stir the oil, which spits in the pot.

Her plan is so clear it numbs me. I feel ashamed to have had so much choice, to have worked nothing out.

She asks about my home. I show some photos on my camera. There are some from the Lake District: the Britannia Arms at Elterwater, the Langdales in the snow. Blessing asks about the snow – whether it's always there. Scrolling further there are photos of a church in Venice, then a shot of some friends in masks, at a New Year party in Udine. They both fall back laughing.

You are dressed as demons!

The last photo is of my mother and brother at Christmas: a table loaded with food and candles. My uncle and cousins are in the background. In the corner of the photo, my aunt is carrying a Christmas pudding, which she has doused in brandy and set alight. We are wearing paper crowns and singing a carol. My aunt had hidden in the pudding, as she did every year, five-pence pieces, which she'd wrapped in greaseproof paper. It was five months ago, but I can recall each detail of the day.

I'm not sure my mother ever understood why I wanted to come here. I knew she was worried; I think because she thought I was throwing my life away. She could see so much future ahead of me. I had a stable job, good prospects if I worked hard. I was twenty-six, starting out in a professional career. I had a roof over my head, friends who were doing the same things, the opportunity to meet people, someone who one day I might settle down with. I earned enough money to live in London and save for a deposit. From the outside, my life made sense.

Although my mother never asked it directly, I could see that she wanted to know what was wrong. There must be something, I think she thought, for me to leave the life I had, to choose instead to come here. But we didn't speak so frankly. I used words that masked what I was really feeling, that put things in a context that was less radical. I wanted an adventure, I said. If I didn't do something like this now, I never would. I could always come back to work at the law firm.

We both knew this would never happen. But we clung to it nonetheless.

I told my boss that I was leaving by phone on Christmas Eve. I was working then on secondment. My boss was a respected litigator and was always sensible and serious. We began the conversation talking about the secondment, what work I was doing, how the team was. I wasn't sure of the right time to explain my plans, so I blurted out in one long sentence that I wanted to leave, where I was going, what I hoped for from the walk. Then, we were talking about deserts, Vodou, insomnia. Why would I want to go into that world? he asked.

Although they say it in different ways, Blessing and Beatrice are asking the same question in the yard; the crickets screeching through the darkness. When they ask of my home, my job, my family, they are trying to understand: Why have you left? Why are you here?

It's the time of evening where we talk less. I wash the pan on the fire, which is now the only light, and smoke a cigarette. I don't tell them that I'd come here because I'd given up back home. That when I went for drinks with colleagues, or went out at weekends, and I smiled, that I felt my smile failing. That, sat at my desk, I'd fall into a kind of paralysis, staring at the screen, waiting for time to pass. I'd got halfway through the year and taken no holiday. I didn't know where to go. I didn't look forward to things. I couldn't sleep. I was bored, which I know is spoiled, as to be bored means there is no struggle, that you don't need to fight for the things that in most places everyone is fighting for. I watched YouTube videos of moving speeches to bring myself to the verge of tears. I got wasted on Friday and Saturday nights, took Valium to put me to sleep. Sometimes I overloaded. I didn't feel unstable exactly, more that I was floating without aim, drifting towards an invisible madness.

I wanted to be away from that. I wanted to be outside. I wanted to lose the roll of fat from my belly. I wanted to have a go at following the ideas in the books I'd scrawled over. I wanted to feel the struggle of walking in the desert. I wanted to get over the things I'd lost. I wanted something to swallow me.

8

The Ashanti people call this region Amansie, which means the Start of Nations.

Ashanti was one of the few places in West Africa I knew when I was a child. I had a *Horrible Histories* book that had cartoons of Ashanti warriors: drummers beating leopard-skin drums, soldiers with spears, mud temples in the jungle. I read adventure stories about explorers travelling through impenetrable forests to reach Ashanti cities of gold. I imagined fighting with the warriors, trekking with the explorers.

Now I am here.

A road of red mud leads from Kade into a valley. The sky is blue-grey at this time, the first light on the horizon. Mists fill the valley. The air is cool. For a long stretch – two or three hours – I see no one. The track moves through thick forest. Huge trees with buttress roots rise beyond the canopy. In places there are swamps. Sticks that look like snakes rise from the water. Lilies cover the pools. The roar of frogs is deafening.

I feel that I'm moving at greater speed than the days before. I sweat heavily, but I stop less to lean on my stick. The pack is less of a strain on my back. I drop the stick to the ground every second step without thinking. The cuts and blisters on my feet, which two days ago left my socks filled with blood, don't trouble me. My breathing is measured. My stomach has settled. I look up more. I have only three days to reach Kumasi.

There are fragments of meteorite scattered in the forests here, a miner told me in Accra. The asteroid hit a million years ago, twenty miles west of here, in what is today dense forest.

In 2004, engineers drilled boreholes into the base of the crater where the asteroid fell, now a freshwater lake. A research team, led by the Curator of the Meteorite Collection at the University of Vienna, examined the sediments recovered from rock. Such was the pressure at the moment the asteroid struck, the geologists wrote, that molten fragments from the asteroid bound together with the broken surface of the earth, forging clasts of new rock, studded with crystals.

An old Ashanti story says that a god once walked from the waters of the lake into which the geologists drilled. The god, who'd taken the form of a man, found an old woman with leprosy who lived alone on the shore. The god made love to the woman, the story says, and the woman had a son. The son, whose name was Twe Adobo, became the father of an *ntoro*, one of the twelve spiritual families which make up the Ashanti world.

The Ashanti are one of several Akan peoples who see these forests as their homeland. In centuries past, Ashanti soldiers raided south along these tracks to do battle with the Denkyira, the Wassa, the Fante, the Fetu. Their merchants carried millet, yams, pineapple and lime to trade with the peoples of the coast. Their priests came here to build shrines among the trees, their miners to dig for gold. The great medieval kingdoms of the Sahara, who ruled in the ninth and tenth centuries from desert cities that were once the richest in the world, built part of their wealth on gold that flowed in the Ashanti rivers and was dug up in this forest earth.

Centuries after Kumbi Saleh, Gao and the other desert capitals lay wasted in the dust, it was rumours of these goldfields – stories told by Muslim traders in the markets of Andalusia and Belém – that triggered the first wave of ships to depart Europe in search of fabled West African mines. The Portuguese sailors who docked on the coast in 1471, one hundred miles south of here, established forts from which to trade and launch their inland expeditions. Soon after, other ships came from Holland, Denmark and Sweden in search of salt with which to cure herring. Later boats came from England and France, for gold and slaves.

By the late seventeenth century, there were dozens of European forts along the shore. Ashanti armies crossed these forest tracks to fight, trade with and defend themselves from the white sailors who had settled there. European merchants brought cloth, gunpowder, tobacco, liquor to sell to the Ashanti kings. The holds of European ships left filled with slaves, gold and ivory.

During those years, elephant roamed these forests. Records kept by the Dutch West India Company, which operated fourteen Gold Coast forts at the start of the eighteenth century, show that the company shipped 1.5 million pounds of ivory in the twenty-six years to 1725. On the basis of these records, the historian Harvey Feinberg calculated that in only fifteen years during this period, ivory hunters were likely to have killed over 12,000 elephants in this small corner of West Africa. Nothing is said of what happened to the carcasses, nor whether the meat was eaten, but it seems likely that at least some of the skins were left to rot among the trees, while the sawn-off tusks were carried by porters on these tracks or taken by canoe on the Pra or Tano rivers to the sea, destined to become ornaments, fine cutlery, and other objects of decoration on English mantlepieces.

No one knows how many thousands of people were walked as slaves across this forest. The slave traders who occupied the Gold Coast forts are estimated to have shipped 880,000 West Africans across the Atlantic in the eighteenth century alone. In total, 10 to 13 million people from Africa are believed to have been captured or killed through the Atlantic slave trade. Countless more died on the journey south, unrecorded in figures anywhere, as they were driven from the markets at Salaga and Kintampo, across this forest to the sea. Some historians suggest that as many as 20 per cent of those who did make it then perished in ports or on ships mid-crossing.

Today, pilgrims from America travel to the Gold Coast to see the places their ancestors left behind. Outside the Ussher and James Forts in Accra, I had watched coaches dropping off church groups from Georgia and Florida, some of whom carried flowers and crosses. In James Fort, the guide explained, slaves were packed into cells so tightly that they were unable to lie or even sit down. There was no flowing water, no natural light beyond the narrow slats, little ventilation. Many died from cholera or malnutrition. Within the upper levels of some forts, there were generous apartments for the white officials who ran the trade. These contained sleeping quarters and sometimes chapels. What is said to be the oldest church in West Africa was built at a Gold Coast slave fort called Elmina, the mine.

Long after the collapse of the slave trade, James Fort was used as a prison. At one point, the guide told us, Charles Taylor, the Liberian president, was interned there while awaiting extradition to the Hague to face war crime charges. Later, the fort housed refugees. Charcoal graffiti remained on some of the cell walls. Among Arabic script, a mural of an American flag, and a portrait of Jesus, those fleeing persecution had written on the stone: 'Darfur', 'Sudan', 'My Home'.

Two hundred years after construction began on the first forts, British soldiers marched north through this forest into Ashanti country. By then, the 1870s, the British had declared the Gold Coast a colony. The Ashanti had fought several wars against the British over the first half of the nineteenth century. In 1824 an almost entire British expedition force was killed on the banks of the Pra River, a short way west of here. Reports from the time say that the skull of the British commander, Sir Charles McCarthy, was set in gold by those who cut off his head, and used by an Ashanti king as a drinking cup.

Fifty years on from that battle, the British army were preparing to march again across this forest. With indentured Fante labourers, they cleared trees and forged rivers to lay the first road from the coast to Kumasi. Black Watch pipers played Highland anthems as they marched. Ashanti war drums beat out. The British won that campaign, now known as the Third Anglo-Ashanti War. As part of the peace treaty, signed in 1874, the British required the Ashanti to pay a duty of 50,000 ounces of gold, and to guarantee that the road across this forest would always remain open.

9

A wide piste of copper mud descends into the trees. The moon is still visible in the pale light. I follow the track into the valley. Here, the mud has churned, and parts of the track are submerged in water. As dawn passes, lemon mists rise from the trees. Clouds settle in the hollows.

It's still early when I reach the first village. The track narrows from the settlement, bordered on either side by climbing shrubs with purple flowers. Children walk the track beside me. They wear yellow uniforms and Disney backpacks, which they carry over their heads to shelter from the rain. One asks my name, and then they all repeat over and over the English they've learned. At the next village, where the children peel off, a man in a suit carrying a bag of yams joins the track. He has no belt, and holds up his trousers with his free hand. The rain passes. Gradually our steps align. As he draws level, I see he has lost all but one of his teeth. Someone has died in Nkwan, he says, gesturing to the bag in his hand. The funeral is today. We fall into silence, walking side by side for an hour.

At each village a new walker joins the track, and a companion departs. At Kwae, a lady with a large bag is walking to catch a ride to Juaso. She wears a headdress of colourful cloth which matches the pattern of her dress. Her sister is at Juaso, she says. Last year her sister's husband left for the cocoa harvest in Côte d'Ivoire, but never returned. No one has news. Her sister has five children. She has work at the market, but it's not enough. One of the children is sick. Once a month she travels to stay with her sister. She does not know how long she will need to go for. Each day, her sister prays for news from Côte d'Ivoire.

Where the track divides, we split. For a long stretch, there's silence. In places streams cross the path. Here, there are copses of bamboo and tall grey trees with leaves like pineapple heads. Ferns grow from the water. The rain creates circles on the surface of the swamp pools.

As children, our mother took my brother and me to Brittany for our summer holiday. Each August she rented a cottage in a hamlet near Plancoët, a few miles off the north Breton coast. There were six cottages on the little road, each run by the gîte company. The cottage we took had a walnut tree in the garden. At night glow-worms lit up the hedges.

We spent most days on the beach at Saint-Jacut-de-la-Mer, a wide bank of sand which, unusually for the region, had a particularly gentle incline between its tide marks, meaning at low tide it was possible to walk as far as three miles from the cliffs out to sea.

The beach was a twenty-minute drive from the hamlet, and from the moment we got in the car, all we thought about were the tides. We asked our mother over and over whether they would be in or out. If she didn't know, we asked the question in different ways, hoping we might trick her into giving a clue. When we arrived, we ran to the cliff edge to see the sea. If the tide was out, we followed the road down to the shore as fast as we could – past the beach latrines and the little bar, which served red wine and waffles – to where the sand seemed to stretch on forever. A far tide meant the best rock pools would be reachable, and we dropped our things, and hurried with our nets to the rocks.

Over the years, we'd come to know the location of the best ledges and the deepest pools. Our legs seemed to remember the routes across the rocks without us thinking. We were very quiet as we explored the ledges. We listened for scrambling and peered, cheeks pressed against the rock, for shining eyes or bubbles in the darkness. We worked to dislodge the crabs with the base of our nets, prodding savagely to force the creatures from their hiding places.

In the far rocks, only reachable when the tide was at its furthest point, there was a pool deeper than the rest. This pool had long rubbery seaweeds and sometimes contained big fish. It was too deep to stand in, and we put on our masks to explore the water. One of us swam to overturn the rocks at the bottom of the pool and the other waited with a net, to trap anything that fled. At the point we overturned the rock, sediment clouded the water. This pool was where we found the largest crabs.

Our mother had to walk out to us across the sand, waving a net in the air, to tell us it was time to go home. Only then did we regain track of time, and make our way back, our buckets filled with the creatures we'd caught. It was as though the whole world outside the rock pools had ceased to exist.

In her biography, there's a picture of Rachel Carson, then a young woman, bent down, pulling back seaweed from a rock pool. By then, sometime in the mid-1950s, she'd written a book about the sea, and would soon publish *Silent Spring*, warning of the disastrous ecological impacts of synthetic pesticides.

As a child, Carson explored the woods and swamps around her Pennsylvania farm. Her biographer, Linda Lear, wrote that her neighbours remembered Carson gathering fossils from the fields and wetlands around the farm. She became fascinated with one large shell in particular, they recalled. She wanted to know what creature the shell had housed, and how it had come to be there, on the banks of the Allegheny River, so far from the ocean. That shell, they said, evolved into a lifelong quest to understand and protect the creatures that lived in the seas, rivers and woods around her.

'It is not half so important to know as to feel,' Carson wrote, years later, reflecting on the meaning of such experiences. 'Once the emotions have been aroused – a sense of the beautiful, the excitement of the new and the unknown, a feeling of sympathy, pity, admiration or love – then we wish for knowledge about the subject of our emotional response. Once found, it has lasting meaning.'

Carson saw contact with nature as a basic need for children, like food or water. As I clutched at ways to change my life, I thought adults were no different. This is an idea in *Walden*. Thoreau believed a person needed nature to be whole. I was drawn to that. Walking through a forest, I thought, could bring out a part of me that lacked. I wanted something like the rock pools: a place where, for a while, everything beyond would cease to exist.

Reaching the city again, I think back to the forest. I got what I came for: mud tracks, trees, miles on my feet. But it wasn't how I thought. I thought the forest would wash out the stress, like in the *shinrin-yoku* papers. I see now it won't work that way. I feel only that it has begun, slowly, to stir up things I'd been hiding from.

10

The path had narrowed and then disappeared to a stream. I followed the water, which seemed the path's logical course. I try to think back to before the stream. I can't pull to mind the trail before that. You'll reach Obugo by the path, the man on the track from Kumeso had said. I liked the sense of following the narrower trail, the feeling of being hemmed in by the forest. It started to rain, so heavily it was hard to see. I got into a different frame of mind then. I put my head down and pushed. When I slipped, I got up without wiping the mud from my hands or legs. I forced myself through thorns, not noticing that my ankles and forearms were covered in blood. Where trees had fallen across the mud, I clambered over them. Climbing over one of the trees was the first moment I sensed I'd gone wrong, seeing how much vegetation had gathered on the fallen trunk. It was curious for the tree to have been like that so long, I thought. I shut the thought down. The path would come out in the right place, I told myself. It became a battle between common sense, stopping and turning back, and the stubbornness to keep going, whatever.

Now, there's nowhere to press on to. The trees have closed the path completely. Everything comes at once: the pain from the cuts, the weariness in my legs, the irritation at the mud on my hands, anger at having gone wrong. I let my stick fall to the mud, shout into the rain at the man from Kumeso, as if it's him, not me, who's responsible. I drain my bottle, and turn back. Retracing my steps is slow. Where before I had a blind drive to go on, now I have no desire, just nowhere else to go, nothing to do but walk back. I clamber over the trees gingerly, curse each time a thorn pulls at my ankle. It takes three hours to reach the place where the path left the track.

At Juaso, forty miles east of Kumasi, I come from the forest to the highway. Here, young men wait with open Bibles where the buses wait to fill up. Others load carcasses onto pick-ups. Blood from the animals runs into the ditches, mixing with the greasy black water. Men surround me with phone cards, lengths of cloth, DVDs. The generators outside the bars burn so loud they drown out the music. Trucks rush by in clouds of smoke.

I count nine dead dogs in the first five miles out of Juaso. Piles of burning rubbish line the verge. Between the fires, there are smashed bottles, segments of watermelon, human excrement in plastic bags. Advertisements for hotels and super-churches rise above the houses. The air is thick with smoke.

I stop for the night at Adako Jachie, a village on the outskirts of the city.

A woman shows me the temple. She wears a crop top, holds a baby at her side, and has a tattoo of a chameleon on her forearm. The temple, in a clearing across which a laundry line hangs, is a small building of stucco mud. Patterns like those carved into my stick are marked on the wood door. The air is musty. Four open rooms give onto a courtyard with a red earth floor. In one of the rooms, two drums, thick with cobwebs, rest against a column. A pile of bones lies beside the drums.

Adinkra mark the walls, Ashanti symbols that tell a story.

The first shows two crocodile heads joined to a single stomach. The crocodiles warn about the dangers of infighting, the woman says. If the crocodiles fight over food, neither will eat.

Beside it is an etching that has lost its shape: a bird pecking its back. The bird is *Sankofa*, a symbol sometimes drawn as a heart, other times as a bird with an egg in its beak. It reminds people to reach back into the past, the woman says, to find there a guide for the future.

The last adinkra we stop beside is a two-legged stool – *Sika Dwa* – which represents the Golden Stool.

The Golden Stool is said to have descended from heaven during the founding of the Ashanti kingdom. At that time, the first king, Osei Tutu, had brought the clans that were scattered through the region together to fight a war with the Denkyira. In the first council of those clans, Tutu's high priest, Anokye, is said to have called the Golden Stool from the sky. Seeing the stool, of solid gold, land in Tutu's lap, the clan chiefs swore allegiance to him as king. This is remembered as the moment the Ashanti kingdom was born. The Ashanti clans defeated the Denkyira, and Anokye advised Tutu to build his capital here, on the forest road that led north to the Sahara. Over the following two centuries, the kingdom that ruled from Kumasi became one of the most powerful states in West Africa.

In the last Anglo-Ashanti War, the British tried to capture the Golden Stool. The British battalion that walked the new road in 1874 burned Kumasi to the ground. From that point, the British required the Ashanti to pay an annual duty. When the Ashanti refused to pay, the British came again to Kumasi. This time the Ashanti king, Agyeman Prempeh, lost the city and was exiled. In negotiations following Kumasi's capture, the British governor, Sir Frederick Hodgson, demanded the Ashanti turn over the Golden Stool, which had been kept since the foundation of Tutu's union. Hodgson told the Ashanti court that the stool was the property of the Queen of England, now supreme ruler of the Ashanti, and that as her envoy he should be sitting on it.

But the British greatly misunderstood the significance of the Golden Stool. Anokye had prophesied that if it were ever lost the Ashanti kingdom would fall forever and its people cease to be. It was a gift from God, said to contain the souls of the living, the dead, and the unborn of the Ashanti. Its loss was unthinkable, and the Ashanti went to war with the British for a final time to protect it. The British eventually took the Ashanti kingdom in 1902 and sent the rest of the Ashanti royal family into exile, but the people of Kumasi never gave up the stool.


11


In the early 1990s – as the US Department of Energy furthered plans for the construction of a nuclear storage facility in Carslbad, New Mexico – the American government convened a panel of experts to devise a way of communicating to future generations, 10,000 years later, not to disturb the ground in that place.

The site at Carslbad had been selected to securely store 850,000 metal drums of radioactive waste generated during the production of nuclear weapons. The government proposed to bury the drums in a chamber 600 metres below ground, on an ancient salt bed beneath the Chihuahuan Desert. The problem facing the panel, which comprised scientists in fields as diverse as architecture, materials science, astronomy, geomorphology and linguistics, was how to make someone see the danger 10,000 years in the future, the final years the waste would be toxic.

The panel produced a report that ran to over 300 pages, assessing what symbols future peoples might be able to understand. They proposed solutions that included the construction of massive earth berms with radar-reflective points, so as to beam the site's presence to the sky; granite monoliths inscribed with warnings in English, Russian, Arabic, Spanish, French, Chinese and Navajo; pictures of radioactive symbols and screaming faces modelled on Munch; fields of giant metal spikes. Each thing constructed would be made of the most durable materials available to humankind, the scientists said, so that the message had the best chance of enduring whatever storms, earthquakes, waves and dusts might come.

In the event that the warnings above ground were misunderstood or destroyed, one group of scientists proposed, there should be time capsules in clay, glass, ceramics and sintered alumina beneath the earth's surface, each containing the message, *Do not dig here*. The most detailed information was to be communicated at the centre of the site, on the walls of a granite bunker.

An atlas on the bunker wall would show the location of all known nuclear waste at the time of interment. Beside it, there would be a periodic table with the radioactive elements highlighted. Maps of the stars – one of the few universal forms of communication, the scientists observed, across human societies over time and place – would show the year of burial and the timeframe in which the site remained dangerous, communicated through the location of the four brightest stars visible from Carslbad: Canopus, Acturus, Vega and the Dogstar, Sirius. Detailed descriptions would be marked in drawings and many languages of what lay below the surface and what would happen if the waste was disturbed. One semiotics specialist, who had considered the same problem a decade before, had suggested a relay system, overseen by what he described as an atomic priesthood: a chain of scientists over time, each responsible to pass on to the next generation, like temple folklore, the obligation to keep the warning language current. As cultures and languages atrophied around the site, he proposed, the warnings would be written and re-written, over and over, never to become lost.

In their reports, the panellists included pictures of great built symbols of the past – Stonehenge, West Kennet Long Barrow, the Sphinx and Pyramids at Giza – all of which were built with effort that is hard to fathom by past communities to tell future generations something we can no longer understand. The panellists observed that the oldest of these structures were less than 5,000 years old: half the time they needed their message to endure.

Much work has been done by archaeologists to try to understand the oldest known human markings, the rock paintings scattered in deserts and mountains where ancient peoples lived, many of which predate the Pyramids by tens of thousands of years. These scholars grapple with the other end of the same problem faced by the Carslbad panellists. What were the ancient peoples trying to say?

At Lascaux, a complex of caves in the Dordogne, the rock walls are marked with vast murals of Palaeolithic animals and geometric patterns. On the shaft which leads into the caves, there's a horse in red and ochre dye, a bison, a hunter with the head of a bird. There are over a thousand figures on the walls of Lascaux: bears, rhinoceros, antelope, aurochs. In the site's most famous cave, the Hall of the Bulls, paintings of stags and horses run in circles across the roof. Among them are four horned bulls, one seventeen feet long.

The men and women who painted the Lascaux caves lived 17,000 years ago in small, semi-nomadic clans. They hunted with bone-tipped spears and foraged for roots, grubs and berries. They were descendants of the first modern humans, who emerged in East Africa 200,000 years ago, and whose children walked across the world.

Painting the caves took great technical skill: extracting iron and manganese pigments from the earth and building scaffolds to reach the cave roofs, as well as, to that point in human history, seemingly unprecedented creativity. But no one knows why the people at Lascaux painted the caves or what they were trying to communicate.

Iégor Reznikoff, a French mathematician who went on to study religious chanting and became a specialist in acoustic archaeology, argued that the peoples who painted the caves at Lascaux were drawn to rocks which reverberated with their chants. Reznikoff mapped the location of

Palaeolithic art within cave complexes in the Pyrenees, the Dordogne and the Urals. He found a correlation between the location of the paintings and the places with the strongest acoustic resonance. He imagined the Palaeolithic peoples following their echoes like a sonar, their chants guiding them through the stone, where they fell into trance, and, inspired, began to paint.

Others have linked the art to the stars. Michael Rappenglück, an historian of astronomy, has argued that the cave paintings at Lascaux were spiritual maps of the sky, what he called cosmovisions. For Rappenglück, the peoples of Lascaux were drawing the seasons of the animals on the cave walls, linking the cycles of birth and rutting of horse and aurochs to patterns they observed in the night skies. In the Hall of the Bulls, the Lascaux painters had drawn six spots above the back of the largest auroch, an image, Rappenglück noted, reminiscent of the Pleiades, associated by many ancient peoples with Taurus. Similar depictions of stars and bulls had been found in other ancient sites, such as on the face of the bulls in the Neolithic settlement of Çatalhöyük, Anatolia. There, Rappenglück observed, the dots drawn on the animals likely represented the Hyades, the sign ancient peoples took for the coming of the rains. At Lascaux, the Pleiades would have become visible for the first time each year, at the end of the summer, in the lead-up to the autumn equinox. Rappenglück believed the animals drawn at Lascaux referenced the mysteries of the night sky, and in this way he saw the caves as an early planetarium.

In a lecture published in his book *The Wayfinders*, the ethno-botanist Wade Davis discusses how the poet Clayton Eshleman, who spent years writing poems about

Lascaux, saw the paintings as a form of mourning. For Eshleman, the murals were an expression of crisis that came at the moment humans transformed from being wild – *thinking like animals* – to having human consciousness. He imagined a precise moment when humans became more human than animal. As the balance tipped, he suggested, it provoked a sense of loss so profound that the cavemen dug up minerals and tried to recreate the world they wanted to remain part of.

Standing in the temple at Adako Jachie, I wonder how long Sankofa and the symbols on the temple wall will remain.

12

The sun is pale at this time, the air dusty. Through the haze, Kumasi is visible ahead. The only people on foot are the children selling lotto tickets and the women with jars of boiled eggs. They gather beside the most potholed sections of road, where the trucks slow and there's time to make a sale. Each passing truck kicks up a cloud of red earth, leaving a trail of dust and fumes. I walk into the city with my scarf pulled across my mouth, as if a desert storm was blowing around me.

I stop at a guesthouse on the Adum Road, down from the old cathedral. The man at reception asks how long I'll stay. I hadn't thought how long I'd be in the city. Since even before I left home, I'd only thought about getting this far, making it to the first waypoint.

The day I left, my mother had asked if she could drive me to the airport. I told her I'd be fine on the bus. I didn't like the thought of that drive. I wanted the moment I closed the door to feel that I was on my way, on my own. Walking the mile to the bus station was the first time I'd walked with my full pack. I felt dread then, feeling the pack's full weight on my shoulders. That weight rooted me. Somehow it killed the expansive thoughts I'd had of crossing forests and mountains, walking across countries. Then, walking to the bus station, I began to think in single miles. Twenty-one miles to Nwasam. Seven hours. Thirty miles to Asamankese. Ten hours. Twenty-two miles to Kade. Eight hours. I ran through each day to Kumasi, calculating in detail the distance and time each would take. That became all I thought about: different ways to tell myself that I would make it to Kumasi.

The journey to Ghana took fifteen hours. A bus to the airport, a stopover in Madrid, another flight. I landed in Accra close to midnight. Stepping from the plane, the heat shocked me. There seemed to be less air to breathe. Vendors and beggars banged on the taxi window at the lights on the way to Darkuman. Everywhere vehicles were blasting their horns. I worried about how I'd find my way from the city on foot. In those days, waiting to leave Accra, I sought out any information I could on my route across the forest to Kumasi. Anyone I met who said they were from the Kumasi region, I probed with questions about the tracks, the villages, any amenities that might be there. To limit my nerves, everything beyond reaching Kumasi faded out.

I follow the man from reception to a room on the second floor. It has plywood walls, a mattress, and no light. There's no running water, the man says, but there are showers and toilets in the ablutions across the street. The showers cost fifteen cents a use, another guest says, leaning into the room. The toilets are five.

Putting down my pack, I feel the distance in my legs and back. It's as though a new weight is in them, as if they've taken something from the ground.

I take each item from my pack and lay it on the floor. In the days before I left home, I arranged the items in my rucksack in different ways to make everything fit. I put the pack on in my room and took a few steps to try to get the balance right. When I had an arrangement I was satisfied with, I unpacked all the items and laid them on the carpet beside the pack. I liked looking at them that way: it made me feel ready.

Months before, I'd written in my list, *No more than forty possessions*. I picked the number out of nowhere then, but it seemed a good limit, something to force me to simplify myself.

I spent hours researching what to take. I wanted to take the old canvas bag my father used on his mountain trips. I still had some of his equipment: an ice axe, crampons, sunglasses with leather side-shields – none of which had been used for years. My father's canvas bag had a heavy metal plate at the back and frayed leather straps. I think he must have bought it in the early seventies. I did some walking with my father's pack; I liked the idea that I would be carrying something of his, but one of the straps broke, and I bought a new rucksack that was half the weight.

I ordered a one-man tent just big enough for me to lie flat in. I could set it without the tarpaulin, so on a warm night I'd have just a net over me. I borrowed other bits of equipment from friends: a sleeping bag, a roll mat, a lightweight pot. I took some things for luck: a cycle cap my friend Mingo gave me; a Lalibela cross tied to a string; and my *shemagh* scarf, which I'd worn on my training runs and hikes, and had become a kind of pendant.

Now, after just a week on the road, dirt and moisture have got into each item, and everything looks worn. I wash my rucksack down in the yard. I make a pile of dirty clothes and note to buy detergent. I patch a tear in my shirt. Kumasi is the last city I'll pass for five months, and I want to get everything set. I note the things I need to buy: new water bottles, to replace the ones from Accra that are dirty and cracked; a secondhand book; pens; salt and sugar to add to my water. I take a cold shower across the street and re-dress the blisters on my feet.

Working through these tasks – mundane things like hosing down the pack, patching up my shirt – feeling each one done, the next one progressing, makes me feel something close to euphoria. I have to tense my arms as I work, to stop my hands shaking from the excess energy the sensation seems to generate. I remember I used to do something similar as I walked to school as a child: I'd turn my hands back and forth, over and over, sometimes with so much movement it must have looked as though I was trying to wriggle free from invisible ropes, too deep in a daydream or internal game to notice.

'It's a dump,' says Mr Kenny, 'but so cheap it's irresistible.' He comes to Kumasi once a year and stays three months at the guest house. 'Mainly there are businessmen,' he says, 'traders from Côte d'Ivoire and Accra, mostly cocoa people. There are few foreigners. The Chinese stay in their own hotels. They come for gold. They have no permits.

You can hear them blowing sides off the hills in the night. They use dynamite. Sometimes there are fights, if they kill livestock, but mostly it just happens. The rivers are filled with chemicals from the mines ... '

He walks slowly, in worn leather sandals, as if he were in a different world to those rushing through the streets. Everyone we pass seems to know Mr Kenny. The ladies boiling noodles on the corners wave to him, the shop-keepers call out, the policemen shake his hand.

'Whatever you're doing in this city', he says, 'it's impor-tant to know the people. The chiefs – the Ashanti kings – you can get nothing done without them. I bring the cloth. All the cloth here – the bright colours – it comes from India. We make things. We have a good factory at home: very big. We bring in the cloth and we sell it and the people in the city, they wear it. But they will only buy it if you take time to talk to them. They are great storytellers. They want to learn about you and your people and tell you their stories. Too many people come here and they don't understand this. They get nowhere.'

We reach the bar where Mr Kenny takes his evening drink. One bottle of beer at 6.30 every evening – never more – and then a bowl of vegetables and rice at the chop house down the hill.

I sit with him at a table on the roadside.

'Perhaps there will be a revolution here,' he says. 'I've seen so many I can see them on people's faces before they happen. Mainly it's inertia that I see. Nothing moving: that creates desperation. I've been on street corners like this – in Kinshasa, Cotonou, Abidjan – the moment before the revolution comes. It's completely still, there's too much slowness, too much boredom for the air, and then it cracks. Most foreigners have packed up by that time. There are a few journalists at the top of the high-rise hotels, peering down at the soldiers. Businesspeople like me have to decide whether to flee and lose everything, or stay and risk getting caught up. People go mad in those moments. The anger becomes uncontrollable.'

He takes a swig of beer, the gold band on his wrist clinking against the glass.

'There are no revolutions in Ghana,' he says. 'But in Kumasi there's the inertia. I see the same things on faces here. Too many people waking up in slum houses, wandering traffic for sales that never come: this is what brings despair.'

I think of a book called *Holy Land*, about a city on the other side of the world.

A city administrator, D. J. Waldie, wrote *Holy Land* about growing up and working in Lakewood, California.

Lakewood was a planned community and town built in the early 1950s on old sugar beet fields in the southeast corner of Los Angeles County. It was the second purpose-built housing suburb in America, constructed to provide affordable housing to Second World War veterans and their families. Seventeen and a half thousand houses were built at a rate of fifty houses a day, according to a local history published by the LA County Library. Lakewood became a blueprint for American suburbia and, in some ways, for what it meant to be modern. The idea of how to live that came from Lakewood spread all over the world.

'My parents bought this house in 1946,' Waldie wrote at the start of his book, less than a year after the war ended, and they felt extraordinarily lucky. Maybe you wouldn't regard a house like mine as a place of pilgrimage, but my parents did. Perhaps their one big move, from the Depression in New York and through the world war to California, had been enough. Their lives afterward seemed to be about that, too – about the idea of enough … More men than just my father have said to me that living here gave them a life made whole and habits that did not make them feel ashamed. They knew what they had found and lost.

Settlements like Lakewood were new when Waldie's parents moved. The buildings and the dreams were fresh. City planners have since modelled tens of thousands of suburbs on Waldie's neighbourhood, housing millions of people. 'Daily life here', Waldie wrote of his suburb, 'has an inertia that people believe in'.

Inertia in the way Mr Kenny is talking about is something I've never experienced. It's a place where there's no work, seeing no way out of poverty, no chance to build a future. It can lead to despair, sometimes to revolution.

Inertia of the kind Waldie wrote about is something I know. It's less immediately harmful than poverty, but it's dangerous. It's spending too much time sat down, watching TV, doing the same thing over and over, often without knowing why. In part it's claustrophobia: too many hours in the same office, the same vehicle, the same living room. Partly it's having so much choice you freeze. More and more people seem to be losing belief in this way of life. At its worst, addiction, depression, loneliness arise from this inertia.

Walking is at least moving. I was nervous when I walked for the first time with my pack to the bus stop, but I knew I needed what was coming. Walking is a way out of inertia.

13

As young children, when we walked in the park by our house, my father held my brother and me on reins to stop us straying too far. The reins had enough give that we could scramble on fallen trees and poke among the bracken. I remember him warning us not to go to close to the swans by the river. Their necks were so powerful, he said, they could topple a grown man. Years later, after we'd packed up our old home and moved to Oxford, my mother would give the same warnings about the swans, when we took walks along the canal. I always thought this odd, as I never heard anyone else give such warnings, and, although I sometimes heard the birds hiss, I knew no instances of swans attacking people. But I liked to hear it all the same, as it was an echo from before.

I don't remember much from that time. I have photos of my father walking with me in the Alps, me in a push-chair, him in a thick jacket and flat cap. We were some-where low down, where there were grasses and gentle tracks. It was sunny and there was no snow on the ground. I can't remember the time itself, but I have the image of the photo, and have generated something in my mind from that. It was spring in Wengen, my mother later said. We always stayed in the same hotel, the Alpenrose. Twenty years after my father died, my mother said, she went back to the Alpenrose: the same family who ran it were there, serving the same muesli. They asked after him, she said, even after all that time had passed.

The clearest memory I have of my father is from a holiday in Normandy. My mother was in the car with my brother. I'd gone with my father into the store to buy fishing nets. My father collapsed on his way to the till, pulling down a postcard stand as he fell. There was a great noise and I dropped the toy I was inspecting, and stared at him on the floor, shaking. I ran from the store, the shop assistant chasing behind.

My mother sometimes tells stories about these times, the years my father was ill. I remember that he lost his hair and always wore a cap. He'd ballooned and his face had become puffy. My mother said that his personality changed too, that he became irritable and lost the awareness of others that he'd had before. He failed at little things, like standing patiently in line at the store, or waiting for other people to serve themselves before helping himself at meals. During Sunday lunches, my mother had to remove the serving bowls from the table, as otherwise, she said, he kept eating and eating, almost grotesquely, as if he'd lost the trigger in his mind which told him to stop. She said, though, that even when there was no good news from the doctors, and they were facing something inevitable, he never stopped showing her hope.

I told my classmates, after he died, that my father had been killed in the Gulf War. I must have been five or six when I told this story. Even years later, sometimes a memory of this surfaces, and still, after so much time, I feel shame at having said that. I don't know why I made up the story about the war. Perhaps six-year-olds will say anything, or it was a way to tell my classmates I believed he was a certain kind of man.

For most of my teens I wasn't aware of thinking about him. He wasn't there, and I was growing up. But I spent time with my father's objects. In the attic, I had his mountaineering equipment, his French horn, volumes of poetry in ancient Greek which, my mother said, he read on the Tube to work. I had his pipe, which he smoked until the early 1980s, but which reminded me more of my grandfather, who smoked his pipe up until he died. And I filled my bedroom with my father's books – mostly paperbacks with worn sleeves, written by writers I didn't yet know – taking them one or two at a time from the front room or the attic, swapping out the story books of my childhood, until my father's books went from the floor to the ceiling of my bedroom. My mother said he spent hours in second-hand bookstores, that he would emerge from the stores having lost all track of time, like a child in a cinema. I forced myself to read his books, to try to get into the worlds he'd passed through, to search out what he took from them.

Sometimes I googled his name to see what was out there. I trawled links and images knowing, in all likelihood, that I'd come across nothing, but letting myself be drawn through the worlds of other John Martineaus. In local newspaper obituaries, archived online, I read the life stories of an oil businessman from Salem, who grew up on a Massachusetts farm and died after a long illness; of a pharmacist from Devil's Lake, North Dakota, who served as a seaman in the Second World War; of a forest ranger from Salt Lake City who fought in the Korean War; of Major Alfred John Martineau, born in Middlesex in 1873, who trained as a surgeon, was initiated in 1913 as a Mason at a lodge in Brighton, and was killed in 1917 by a bullet to the brain while on reconnaissance in the Bois de Riaumont. I passed through the LinkedIn, Myspace and Facebook profiles of John Martineaus of no relation to me; local news reports from Canada, Australia, South Africa; covers of books on cosmology and crop circles, and biographies of persons of note, such as the *Life and Correspondence of Sir Bartle Frere*, published in 1895 by a John Martineau, whom I presumed to be a historian, about a British colonial administrator, who was Governor of Bombay in the 1860s, and then posted to Southern Africa, where he presented an ultimatum to the Zulu king, Cetshwayo kaMpande, before overseeing the invasion of Zululand of 1879. I followed these pathways as though I was daydreaming, finding myself in the midst of strange stories, grasping for something unreachable.

I didn't come here with these things in mind. They are memories I haven't thought of in years. But as I walk, they are there, and they come up. In them, I see the void I've never been able to fill.

14

Every six weeks people in Kumasi celebrate the Adae, a festival of thanks for the ancestors.

The temple in which I attend the ceremony is on a rock outcrop in the Medoma township, in the north of the city. Two stone eagles stand either side of the gates, engraved with the words *Powers and Wonders*. Hundreds of people wait in the temple car park, where gazebos and flood lights have been set up.

Girish, an anthropologist I met in the city, takes me to the office of the priest, Nana Abass. The office smells faintly of palm oil. Abass sits in white robes behind a desk. He has a close-shaved head and a thumb of red dye on his forehead. He speaks slowly. He asks what I'm doing with my life, what I'm doing in Ghana. He explains about the Adae and what will happen.

Abass has been the priest here since the 1980s. He built the shrine slowly, rising to prominence after he found aquifers beneath the townships of Medoma and Agona. He said spirits led him to the water. The discoveries transformed the settlements, giving thousands access to fresh water for the first time. Abass is known here as the Well-Finder.

His story is full of magic. He says there were signs he'd been chosen to serve the spirits shortly after he was born. Forest spirits took him as a child from the fields where his mother was working. His mother only found him after she left offerings beneath a tree. He came back smeared with white mud, his ankles bound with reeds.

At school Abass saw children no one else could see. His mother took him to the grove at Tano, the shrine I'm walking to. The priest told her that her son was destined to serve the spirits. Abass was sent to live with his father's family, out of Ashanti lands, to escape them.

In the 1970s he returned to Kumasi, then a young man. One night he was driving his taxi and the car doors began to slam open and shut. A figure carrying a sword appeared in the seat beside him. Terrified, he went to an imam for help. The imam instructed him to convert to Islam, and the visions stopped.

One day in 1983 his taxi caught fire. He saw figures in the flames. He returned to the imam, who said he was under a spell. The imam instructed him to go to a shrine in the far north of Ghana to have the spell lifted. As he entered the shrine house it burst into flames. The priest told him there was nothing he could do: he must follow the path he was destined for. He experienced spirit possession and gave in. The spirits carried him to the forest to be initiated. When he returned to Kumasi, they left him on top of the tallest tree in Medoma, telling him to build his temple on the rocks beneath.

The ceremony starts near midnight beside the rocks beneath the tree. Abass's attendants mark the ground with maize flour. The crowd has swelled. Behind the old men, who sit in the front in robes with gold sandals and canes, there are young men in basketball shirts, women in white cloth, children running and shouting. The drums begin and the crowd quiets. The first dancer to arrive is a child, a boy of no more than seven or eight. The child is Abass's youngest son, the lady beside me says. He wears a grass skirt and white beads around his neck. An attendant sprays perfume at his feet, and the mist from the spray lingers in the floodlight. The crowd drops to its knees as the child moves towards the drums.

Most ceremonies here start with drums. Dancing is so closely connected here with spirituality that in some Akan languages the words for 'to dance' and 'to prophesy' are the same. In Ewe, spoken in western Ghana, the word 'to dance' means literally 'to spin the sun'.

The drumming intensifies, and Abass comes from the shrine house. He wears a skullcap and carries a stick. At first he walks slowly. As he reaches the centre of the crowd he begins to move more fluidly, swaying, faster and faster, until the flaps of the robe beneath his arms spread as if caught in the wind. He takes off the robe and continues spinning. An attendant throws a cloak to the air. The cloak drops over his head onto his frame. The change is to show that a spirit is with him. The woman beside me says the spirit's name is *Adiako*, which means 'if you do not eat what you are used to you will vomit.'

At one time spirit possession was an almost universal human experience. A study on trance in 488 societies from around the world, published in 1968, found that trancing happened in over 90 per cent of them. The author concluded that trancing was a 'psycho-biological capacity available to all'. It's most common today in religious contexts: Sufis hitting *fana* ('passing away'), Pentecostals falling out, Japanese mystics reaching *nembutsu* (chanting to seek the mindfulness of Buddha), Vodou possession: all are different ways to step out of oneself and become, for a time, something else.

In ancient Greece, at the time of the autumn equinox, initiates of the cults of Demeter and Persephone sacrificed suckling pigs and bathed in the sea at Phalerum, as they began what remains the most famous of all altered-state rituals. Swinging branches as they walked, they processed from Athens along the Sacred Way to Eleusis. There, lit by the lights of burning torches, they held all-night vigils in which they danced, drank and acted out Persephone's fall and rise from the underworld. The ceremonies of the Eleusinian Mysteries finished with dancing on the Rharian Field, where, the myth of Demeter says, humanity's first seed of grain was sown.

The Greeks practised the Mysteries for 2,000 years. What was revealed to the participants by the priests, who were sworn never to speak of the climax, remains unknown. In the moment before the ceremony's climax, Plutarch wrote, initiates were seen convulsing, shivering and sweating. The experience was so profound, Cicero said, that those who took part returned to 'the very beginnings of life', a place where they gained 'the power not only to live happily, but also to die with a better hope'.

It's said the Mysteries grew from ancient pre-Greek pagan rites, that rituals emerged from them whose remnants are still followed across the world in Catholic and Orthodox churches, and pagan-inspired festivals like Burning Man. From the little knowledge modern people have of what happened, the format of the Mysteries seemed structured to facilitate the onset of altered states. The pilgrimage from the cemetery, the burning torches at Demeter's sanctuary, the singing and the dancing, the acting out of ancient stories: all were a sequence that could help carry the participant to a place where attachment to their self and normal state of consciousness fell away. There's been much speculation about the role played by the ritual drink, *kykeon*, in the ceremony. Archaeologists, ethnobotanists, pharmacologists, neuroscientists and ancient historians have all sought the formula, speculating that it contained a potent psychoactive compound, capable of bringing the ancient worshippers to ecstasy.

Whatever the role of *kykeon* in the mystical experiences of those who took part, other elements of the Eleusinian rites – chanting, dancing, drumming – can all be portals into an altered state of consciousness. And as I've begun to see, walking too can be a way into trance.

'The action or rhythm of walking', Meister Eckhart wrote in the thirteenth century of the Sufi practice of *siyahat*, was used by mystics 'as a technique for dissolving the attachment of the world and allowing men to lose themselves in God. The aim of the dervish was to become a "dead man walking"; one whose body stays alive on the earth yet whose soul is already in heaven.'

Seven centuries later, writing about the ritual walks of Australia's first peoples, Bruce Chatwin quoted Eckhart's passage. The Songlines about which Chatwin wrote are tracks which follow routes the creator ancestors took during the Dreamtime, when the first human beings emerged on the earth. The paths taken by the creators are mapped by songs which describe the hills, trees and waterholes along the path. It's said that experienced Songline walkers are able to reach such a state of concentration that they can navigate hundreds of miles of desert with no more than their songs.

In an account of the Himalayan pilgrimage he undertook in 1947, the Buddhist monk, Anagarika Govinda, described monasteries in the old Tsang province of Tibet in which monks sought the state of *lung-gom-pa*, a meditative practice said to enable a mystical trance-running. The monks lived as hermits for a period of up to nine years, Govinda wrote, in complete solitude, focusing only on their breathing. This training, the stories of the *lung-gom-pa* say, allowed the monks to reach a trance-like state through which they achieved new physical capability. 'It is said that his body by that time has become so light', Govinda wrote of the monks, 'that he can move with the speed of a galloping horse, while hardly touching the ground'. In this trance, the *lung-gom-pa* monks were said to be able to run for forty-eight hours without rest, covering up to 200 miles a day.

'I jumped from boulder to boulder,' Govinda remembered as he found something like the *lung-gom-pa* state one night on a mountain trail, 'without ever slipping or missing a foothold … I realised that a strange force had taken over, a consciousness that was no more guided by my eyes or my brain. My limbs moved as in a trance … Even my own body had become distant, quasi-detached from my willpower.'

In Japan, at a Tendai temple on Mount Hiei, north Kyoto, monks take a pilgrimage called *kaihōgyō*, 'circling the mountain'. The first stage of the pilgrimage involves one hundred days of mountain running, which all monks must pass through to become a novice of the order. The second stage, to which few graduate, comprises six further years of mountain running, with the daily distances lengthening each year. In the ritual's final year, the monks run forty-eight miles a day for a hundred days. Through the daily ritual of the run, *kaihōgyō* pilgrims seek self-annihilation and enlightenment. The pilgrimage is said to have grown from the practice of a ninth-century mystic, Soo, who walked the mountain until he fell into trance beside a waterfall. There, he saw visions of the Buddhist god, Fudo Myoo.

'Walking itself is the intentional act closest to the unwilled rhythms of the body,' Rebecca Solnit wrote in her history of walking. As I've got into the walk, and the anxiety of how far I have to go has retreated, I've begun to get what Solnit says. For periods, I feel like I'm falling back into a state I haven't encountered for years, that the motion of the walk is letting my mind run, opening up something like a dream. Solnit described this as a kind of alignment, a bringing together of mind, body and world. In walking they become, she wrote, 'three characters finally in conversation together, three notes suddenly making a chord'. Seen in that way, the mental state accessed deep in a walk is not so different to what the Greeks sought at Eleusis, or what the Ashanti dancers strive for here.

Abass dances for an hour as *Adiako*. Through the night he emerges in fresh robes, inhabited by different spirits. At one point he is in black, holding a cane. Now he is *Afeyke*, the joker. He wears a bed cap and a dress of torn cloth covered with banknotes stuck on with pins. Anyone who reaches for the money will go mad, the lady beside me says.

The energy grows as the night draws on. The crowd throws eggs at *Afeyke*'s feet as offerings. Every few minutes he stops to speak, talking in riddles; telling stories of fish dropping from the sky, cattle walking from the sea, shoots of maize growing to trees as tall as towers. At points he is serious, warning of the dangers of fighting, of taking on debt, of failing to look after the needy.

It's 4 a.m. Children sleep in their mothers' slings. The old men watch on impassively. With *Afeyke*'s coming, others join the dance. Some let go, their eyes rolling to the backs of their heads. Others fall to the floor, shaking as if charged with an electric current.

The mind in trance seems to pass into a state of extreme calm. During trance, the most ancient brain region – the limbic system – becomes dominant. It is thought that increased activity in this region enables sub- or unconscious thoughts to rise to the surface, which can help a person gain insight. Parts of the brain responsible for executive control relax. At the same time, serotonin inhibition falls away, flooding the body with feelings of ecstasy.

Some research goes as far to suggest that trancing is a psychological need. Nathaniel Kleitman, who pioneered sleep research in the 1930s, proposed that when we're awake, we pass through regular trance-like phases, where our minds disconnect from the world in front of us and engage in hyper-imaginative thought. Kleitman saw these waking cycles as mirroring Rapid Eye Movement sleep cycles, which we pass through every ninety minutes during the night and are when we dream. In the industrialised world, people suppress these waking trance-like episodes. Continually moving from one distraction to another, we miss out on important imaginative and restorative thought.

At first light the call to prayer sounds from the Medoma mosques. We follow Nana Abass to the shrine houses on the rocks. The rocks are steep, and the old go down on their bums and hands. I follow slowly behind. The air is still warm. It smells of perfume and of the sweat which is still visible on the foreheads of those around me. For the first time in many hours, I realise, there are no drums. The calls to prayer have faded out and it's peaceful. At the end of the line, Abass stands beneath a floodlight. He gives us each a bucket. He tells us to pour the water over our heads, that it will help wash away sadness. We file past the shrine in a long line, drenched.

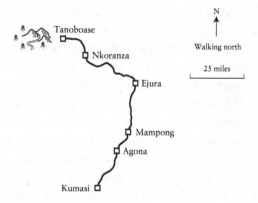

*To a forest grove at the source of the Tano River, site of an Akan shrine and a monastery. The road north from Kumasi to Tano is 120 miles, crossing the Awura Forest, and the old Ashanti towns of Mampong and Ejura.*

When Mark Nelson first crossed through the airlock, into the test module of the greenhouse that was to be his home for twenty-four months, he said the sensation of being in a new world hit him immediately. Because of the thicker air, he recalled, breathing was itself a different experience. And in an instant his body could feel, he said, something more nourishing in that air, that he was connecting – metabolically – with everything around him.

The world into which he was preparing to walk – a vast structure of glass and steel, covering three acres of Arkansas desert – enclosed 3,800 plant and animal species. The building had been devised in the 1980s, following earlier Soviet experiments, to house an environment completely shut off from the outside world. The project would allow, it was hoped, humans to better understand the interrelationships between the planet's living systems: it was to be a second earth, in a laboratory. It would be the first step in seeing how humans might colonise a new world in space.

Mark Nelson was one of eight people selected to live within and tend the world in the greenhouse, known as Biosphere 2. Like astronauts preparing for a mission, the crew members underwent extensive evaluation, medical training and, so far as possible, simulations of the environments and situations they would face in their new home. Once inside the biosphere, they would be completely self-sufficient: they'd grow, harvest and cook their own food, process their own waste, and work to ensure the delicate balance of life was maintained within the greenhouse, so they and the life forms around them would survive.

The first task of each day, Nelson wrote, was to review the daily report of the biosphere's atmospheric conditions, which showed the levels of oxygen, carbon dioxide and trace gases in the air. The architects who designed the facility did so with the goal of making the structure completely airtight. The slightest change in the air's gas levels, Nelson said, could destroy the project or, worse, make the air unbreathable and endanger their lives.

Beyond the human habitat where the crew ate, slept and carried out research, the biosphere contained an area for intensive agriculture: half an acre on which the crew grew crops without pesticides or chemical fertilisers; a small zone for livestock; and the wilderness biomes, which comprised a miniature desert, an ocean and coral reef, a freshwater marsh, a mangrove forest, a savannah, a thorn scrub and a rainforest.

The crew spent a significant portion of their time tending the biomes: clearing the algae from the reefs to prevent the water becoming too acidic, for example, or cutting by scythe the savannah grasses to keep them at natural levels. According to Nelson's account, in addition to biome management, each crew member spent three to four hours a day tending the farm, on which they grew rice, sweet potato, plantain, beans, beets and all kinds of green vegetables. In the livestock area, they raised a small number of goats, pigs and chickens, which they butchered themselves, and ate on special occasions.

As the project progressed, and the crew had been inside for months, and then a year, the Biospherians – as the crew became known – grew to be the subject of intense media attention. Nelson recalled how significant time came to be taken up with interviews. In this respect, elements of the experiment resembled an early *Big Brother*, with endless questions, via video link, as to how long the crew members could survive inside, and speculation about the relationships between the eight, including whether a baby might be born in the high-tech forest world behind the glass.

The crew lasted two years in the biosphere. Over that time the oxygen levels in the air had slowly depleted, down from normal levels on the day the crew first passed through the airlock, to just 14 per cent on their last, the equivalent of living at 15,000 feet above sea level. Some of the crew had begun to exhibit symptoms resembling altitude sickness. Coming back through the airlock, Nelson recalled, breathing the new air was again like being in a different word. Suddenly, he said, it was no longer a struggle to walk.

Among the many challenges the crew faced inside, one was the spread of the vines from the rainforest. Many jungle creatures lived in the forest biome – frogs, lizards, snakes, even bush-babies – but, alongside outbreaks of ants and roaches, it was the vines which grew uncontrollably from the tropical trees that most threatened the balance of life in the biosphere. From Nelson's account – which includes descriptions of how the vines put down roots wherever they spread, and how the crew worked to tear them up as they spread across the mangroves and the savannah – it was possible to imagine how the vines, if left untended, could have spread across the ocean pool, down into the paddies and the plots of beets, through the cages of the livestock, and under the doors of the Biospherians' sleeping quarters. In such a way, the vines would have grown to cover every panel of the structure, blocking out the light for all the creatures, until they finally cracked the glass, and broke out into the desert.

There was, on the south Cornish coast, in the first half of the twentieth century, a rainforest in a garden which, after falling into neglect during the First World War, spread in something like the way I imagined the biosphere vines. That rainforest – of ferns, bamboo and dozens of rare tropical trees – was one of several areas which made up the 1,000-acre garden of the estate of Heligan House, seat of the Tremayne family since the sixteenth century.

It had been Jack Tremayne – when in the 1890s he returned to Heligan to tend to his elderly father, John – who oversaw the creation of the rainforest. According to Tim Smit, who went on to lead the restoration of the garden at Heligan a century later, Jack Tremayne introduced to his rainforest palms from the Yangtse, ferns from New South Wales, black pine from Japan and yew trees from New Zealand, together with beds of bamboo and swamp pools which he dug into the Cornish soil.

'We felt like explorers coming on a lost world,' Smit recalled of the day they re-entered Jack Tremayne's rainforest in February 1990. The rainforest, together with the vinery, the vegetable garden, the Italian garden, the beehives and the various outhouses which dotted the estate gardens, hadn't been tended since the latter stages of the Great War, when the Heligan gardeners had gone to the Western Front, many never to return. The garden Smit entered was a ruin. Vegetation had taken over every area of the once meticulously managed estate. The shells of fountains, verandas and greenhouses lay concealed beneath brambles and vines. A layer of lichen and moss, Smit recalled, had smothered the rainforest floor, and the ferns and bamboo that Jack Tremayne had carefully planted were lost beneath a wild forest of ash and sycamore.

It took Smit, John Nelson, his partner on the restoration, and a vast team of labourers and volunteers years to clear the acres of vegetation that had overcome the gardens at Heligan. Their vision was to restore the gardens to what Jack Tremayne and his ancestors had envisaged: to make operational again the orchards, the manure heating systems, the hydraulic rams; to return to life the vegetable garden; to fill the hives with bees; to replant the vinery, the beds of exotic flowers, the rainforest. The Lost Gardens of Heligan, with the rainforest – many of its original ferns and trees re-nurtured to life – were opened to the public for the first time in the early nineties, with the last sections to be restored opened in 1997. Each year since, tens of thousands of people have visited, to see the exotic plants and the trees, and to hear the story of how the wild forest took over and was pulled back to reveal the hidden garden.

It is, in some rare instances, people who turn the other way, and spread like the vines, pushing on and on into the forest, further and further from the human world. It was this path which Karp and Akulina Lykov took in 1936, when they fled into the forests of south Siberia.

Forty years after Karp and Akulina Lykov had first disappeared into the trees, with their two infant children, Savin and Natalia, a pilot, circling a remote region of the southern taiga, caught sight of a clearing, a strange thing 250 kilometres from the nearest human settlement. Passing back and forth over the spot, the pilot saw signs of human life: trees cleared and rudimentary trenches dug into the soil. Later, the geologists the pilot had set down went on foot to investigate. They found, on the banks of a stream, a hut of blackened wood. An old man, barefoot and in rags, came out from the shelter. Two women emerged behind him.

Over the coming weeks, the old man and his family recounted their story. The man had left his village after a government soldier shot his brother. Lykov and his family were members of the Old Believers, an orthodox sect outlawed under the Soviets. Seeing the body of his murdered brother, Karp Lykov gathered his family and set out into the woods, over the following decade pushing deeper and deeper into the forest.

Such was remoteness of their new home that before the day the geologists arrived in the summer of 1978, neither of the Lykovs' two further children – Agafia and Dmitry, both born in the forest – had ever seen a human outside of their family group. In those intervening decades, the family survived, according to the account of the Lykovs' story, entirely from the land. They had carried with them seeds when they first fled into the forest, and they lived primarily off potatoes, from which they made a primitive black bread, turnips, pea pods and rye, which they ate as porridge on special occasions. During the summer months they foraged for mushrooms, bilberries and currants. They gathered pine cones from the tops of the trees and tapped birch trees for sap. They fished in the nearby river, standing barefoot in the icy water for hours. They hunted using traps, occasionally catching elk or Siberian deer, which they cut to strips and dried. Some years they went without meat. When they got sick, they prepared tree fungus with boiling water, or took preparations of rhubarb root and nettles. They stored their food as best they could, digging traps to catch raiding bears, and cutting their potatoes into discs, which they dried in the sun, to help them last years. For decades they didn't eat salt: it was this, of all things, that Karp Lykov said had been the hardest of everything they'd foregone in their forty years in the forest.

For most of their needs they made do with what the forest provided. For clothes, the Lykovs grew hemp, from which they derived a coarse thread. They made shoes from birch bark, before Savin learned to tan leather from the hides of the few animals they caught. Most of each day was spent on the tasks to keep themselves sustained.

For entertainment, they recounted their dreams. They were meticulous about recording each day, month and year, so that they would never miss the religious holidays they observed as if a matter of life or death. Some winters the Lykovs lived close to famine. In 1961, when Akulina starved to death, the family was reduced to eating bark and the leather from their shoes.

Soon after the Lykovs re-established contact with the outside world – still living in their forest dwelling – three of Karp and Akulina's children passed away in quick succession: Savin and Natalia of suspected kidney failure; Dmitry of pneumonia. Karp died in 1988. It was as if, with the door to the forest suddenly re-opened, life somehow drained from the Lykovs. Only Agafia survived, and continued to live, isolated, in the Lykov forest homestead. Twenty-five years after her father's death, in 2013, a team from *Vice* travelled to interview her. The journalists found Agafia still living in the same location, a cabin overlooking the Erinat River, growing her own food. She had left the forest five times in her life, the article reported, once on a tour of the Soviet Union in the mid-1980s, soon after the Lykovs' story had spread and they'd become folk heroes. She told the journalist that though life in the taiga was hard, she couldn't leave, as drinking anything other than water from the Erinat River that flowed past her hut made her sick, and she found it hard to breathe the air outside the forest.

16

Beyond the last of the dwellings, men in torn shirts work the ground with machetes. They gather for shade beneath the trees. The track crosses forest and swamp. Vast lilies with wide, flat leaves float on pools of green water. Dragonflies come from flowers at the water's edge. Vines hang from the trees and red birds shriek in the leaves. Where the track narrows, the vines grow thickly, and the tops of the trees have twined together, so it's like walking through a tunnel. At the point the track opens out in the distance, there's a circle of white light.

A few miles out of Ejura, it begins to rain. The rain intensifies, until a film of water runs over the path. Currents froth where the water encounters vegetation. In the wet, the bright forest colours are lost: there's just the dulled green of the leaves, the brown of the path, the blue-clear of the water which washes through everything. My eyes sting with the salt from my temples. I can see only a few metres ahead.

As children, sometimes my brother and I heard storms in the woods around our grandmother's house. We always went to the woods with my grandmother's dog, a sheep-dog called Tan, carrying sticks, which we held like staffs. We walked to the end of the garden, into the fields beyond, out of sight of the house. At the edge of the far field, where it met the woods, there was a stream. We walked along it, dipping our sticks into the black mud. Sometimes we built dens in the trees. If we heard thunder, or we sensed the sky darken too quickly, we dropped our sticks and ran back through the fields to the house, stumbling as the rain began. Although we were never more than a mile from the back door, we felt, in the trees beside the stream, that we were at the edge of the world.

I can only see fragments of those woods now: winter bracken that seemed to stretch forever; sand tracks through blue heather; saplings in protective sheaths on the bluffs; and the occasional vast tree, with thick, gnarled branches and a hollowed trunk, large enough for us to walk into, in which we investigated mushrooms and the insects that occupied the cold, damp bark. I sometimes saw faces or creatures in those trees as we walked. Even though I knew these were only in my mind, I drew closer to my brother on the track.

'Superstitious natives believed that the ground often shook,' the Roman poet Lucan wrote of the Sacred Grove of Marseilles in AD 61. Lucan described altars among the trees, which he said were sprayed with blood. He told stories, too – relayed to him by local people – of strange happenings in those woods: yew trees miraculously standing again after being felled; snakes curled among the roots of giant oaks; trunks set alight that held flames without the wood burning.

Across northern Europe, as in the forests here, there's a deep history of mystical forest stories. Perhaps it's why, even now, I still see things in the trees, still sometimes quicken my pace for no good reason. It's why, too, I think, the saleswomen who give me oranges on the roadside offer warnings. The forest road they point to fills with wild animals, demons, bandits.

Tacitus, writing twenty years after Lucan, described Roman solders swimming beside their horses as they crossed the channel from the Welsh beaches to Anglesey. As the soldiers approached, he wrote, they saw a circle of Druids on the sand, in black robes, with wild white hair, arms raised to the sky. The soldiers destroyed the groves the Druids tended. In some of the forest shrines, Tacitus wrote – perhaps embellishing for effect – the soldiers found human entrails hanging from the trees.

Across the Irish Sea from Anglesey, in County Carlow, on the banks of the River Barrow, there's said to have stood a great yew tree – the Yew of Ross – worshipped by local people. It fell, according to an account of the life of a local saint, after monks prayed and fasted. The monks distributed planks from the tree's trunk, to be used as beams in the grey-stoned churches and monasteries that had begun to emerge across Ireland's forests and valleys. The ancient wood, it was believed, would fill the new houses of worship with its power.

Across Ireland and the British Isles at the time, early Celtic peoples believed yew trees were carried from the Otherworld, that they could resuscitate the dead. Celtic Druids cut their staffs from yew wood. The power English people once associated with yew trees is the reason they're so often found in graveyards.

Oaks, which at one time covered Britain, were part of national legend. They've given refuge to fleeing kings, been inhabited by thunder gods, turned into monsters. At Glastonbury Tor, there are two oaks over 2,000 years old called Gog and Magog. The trees take their names from the last two members of a mythical race of giants that lived on the British Isles and were slaughtered by the armies of Brutus of Troy, Britain's mythical founding king. Gog and Magog are said to have morphed into these oaks.

In West Africa, forest myths often concerned silk-cotton trees. In parts of Benin, east of here, children learned that they were descended from silk cottons, that the hearts of children yet to be born dwelt in the leaves. Traditional priests are known as *amawato*, observers of the plants. In some communities, it was the custom to offer sacrifices to forest spirits before felling a silk cotton. Children learned that these trees felt pain.

In Ashanti country, many forest stories were about the *Mmoatia*. It was the *Mmoatia* who took Nana Abass when he was a child and left him on top of the tree in Medoma. The *Mmoatia* were sometimes said to be guardians of all forest folklore. The spider *Anansi*, those stories said, once set a trap to capture the *Mmoatia*'s stories. Anansi carved a doll out of wood from a gum tree, which he covered in silk, and left to hang from a branch, over a bowl filled with the *Mmoatia*'s favourite food. The *Mmoatia* ate the food and stretched out a hand to thank the hanging doll. Her hand became stuck in the sticky silk. The spider dropped from the branches and spun more silk around her, taking from the *Mmoatia* all the stories of the forest. Later, Anansi is said to have stored the knowledge he obtained in a calabash, which he buried beneath a silk cotton.

Before I came to West Africa, I met with my uncle, a geologist who spent much of his life mining in this region. He warned me to take care in northern Ghana. One of the stories he told was about protests over the felling of a tree at a mine near Bolgatanga. He said local people went mad as the tree was chopped down, some reacting violently, as they believed the tree was a god. As my uncle told the story and I heard it, we were both thinking how irrational this reaction was. Walking now, I remember my uncle's story, and the protesters' reaction no longer seems crazy.

Ahead, where the forest has been cut back, piles of palm fruit lie beside a ditch. A woman in an apron and headcloth sits before a blackened cauldron, stirring oil. Curls of smoke hang in the wet air. In many places I've passed, the forest has been burned to make way for palm and cocoa, or trees pulled down to clear space to dig for gold. Ghana lost 90 per cent of its forest in the twentieth century. A thousand square kilometres have been felled each year since.

'The point is not to ask or suggest which perspective is right or wrong,' Wade Davis said in one of his *Wayfinders* lectures:

> Is the forest mere cellulose and board feet? Was it truly the domain of the spirits? Is a mountain a sacred place? Does a river really follow the ancestral path of an anaconda? Who is to say? Ultimately these are not the important questions. What matters is the potency of a belief, the manner in which a conviction plays out in the day-to-day lives of a people. ... A child raised to believe that a mountain is the abode of a protective spirit will be a profoundly different human being from a youth brought up to believe that a mountain is an inert mass of rock ready to be mined.

In most places now, tree worship is seen as primitive. But walking, I think about the stories our ancestors created about the forests. The *Mmoatia*, the giants at Glastonbury, the spirits in the silk cottons or the power of the yews: the things which led the villagers at the mine at Bolgatanga to fight, and which lead the women who sell oranges on the roadside to warn me of the dangers of the woods – for whatever reason the stories emerged, all ended up protecting the forest.

The peoples who live near the grove at Tano – now thirty miles away – believed it to be the site of the beginning of the world. The forest became sacred, and it was always forbidden to fell trees or hunt there. Without the Biosphere's glass, or the taiga's remoteness, the Tano story created its own shield. Inside, the forest has remained untouched since the earliest human settlement.

The road rises up the escarpment back into the forest. Off the track, creepers climb from beds of copper earth. It's not yet fully light, and among the leaves the air is damp. Torch lilies grow at the roots. The roots are the colour of elephant hide and buttressed like bridge feet. Shoots of water pour from gashes in the stone. Moths swarm around me. They are big as birds.

Each time the road winds back into the forest, I feel lifted. Perhaps this is the shade, maybe that there is just more happening than in the scrub. A forest is more interesting than cleared land because there is more life to look at.

It's six hours to Tano. A track of red mud weaves over gentle rises and across rust streams. The forest is thick. Women pass barefoot, babies on their backs and twenty-litre water cans on their heads. The men head to their plots with machetes. Flocks of yellow and green birds cut across the sky. The sound of water in the trees is continuous.

The grove at Tano is off a red dirt road, a mile east of the village of Tanoboase. It's marked with a sign painted 'Sacred Grove' in bright yellow letters. Within the grove boundaries, there are vast sand rocks, some fifty feet high. Among them is the spring which feeds the Tano River.

The Ashanti traditionally believe the site is home to Taakora, the father god. For the Abron, a local people who also trace roots to Tano, this was the place of *kanky-erekyere*: the very beginning.

An Abron creation story holds that the first ancestors – *the children of red earth* – came from a hole in the ground and settled in the lands beside these rocks. Soon after building their homes, a spirit came to the wife of the community's great hunter. She gathered her people and led them to the rocks. God spoke through her, telling them that the stone had been at the site before he created heaven and earth. As she spoke, water ran from the earth beside the rock. Her people watched as the river drained across the country to the sea.

I sit for a while on the rocks. It's the cooler part of the day, an hour before dusk. The light is softer, the air warm, the mosquitoes not yet out. I stay on the rocks until the sun falls, then follow a path through the forest to the monastery.

The Tanoboase monastery is at the bottom of a red dirt track, in a tree-walled compound. A slight man in white robes greets me at the gates. His name is Brother Gabriel, he says. He leads me through an orchard, strewn with boulders, to the main abbey buildings. A line of cells gives onto the central lawn. He shows me to a cell. It has a bed, a writing table and a bucket for washing. The daily routine is pinned on a board above the desk.

0430: Rise.

0445: Vigils.

0600: Morning prayer.

0645: Mass.

0730: Breakfast.

0810: Mid-morning prayer, followed by manual work or studies.

1230: Midday prayer.

1245: Dinner and siesta.

1445: Afternoon prayer, followed by manual work or studies.

1730: Evening prayer, followed by time for silent prayer.
1830: Supper.
1945: Compline.
2030: Great Silence. Retire to bed.

Supper is kenkey – fermented maize dough – with tomato and okra. We eat in silence, while one of the monks reads aloud from a book on Sufi poetry. He begins with a section about Farid ud-Din Attar, a twelfth-century poet from Nishapur, in present-day Iran. No one knows how Attar learned to write, the monk reads, nor how he encountered Sufism. In some stories, Attar is said to have left his trade as a pharmacist, travelling to Basra, Mecca, Damascus, as far even as India. It's possible he met Sufi teachers on his journey. He became an initiate, poet and mystic.

The second part of the reading is about Attar's poem, *The Conference of the Birds*. The birds are gathered together and told by the wise hoopoe that they are to go on a quest to find their king, the Simorgh. On their journey, they will cross seven valleys, each representing a barrier to enlightenment. The birds go on a perilous journey. Many die. With each valley, the birds shed a layer of attachment to things they do not need. Beyond the seventh valley – the Valley of Annihilation – they reach the home of the Simorgh. They find there only a mirror and their own reflections. In crossing the valleys, the monk relates, the birds have become what they were seeking. They have become like drops in an ocean, one with everything.

Brother Gabriel says there's a reading each night, that the evening meal is always taken in silence.

He has been at the monastery for seventeen years. The community is close to self-sufficient. In the kitchen garden, the monks grow yam, maize, plantain and cassava, alongside a patch for green vegetables and another for herbs. There's an orchard for fruit and an apiary. Beyond the walls, the monks operate a farm where they harvest cashew nuts, moringa and cinnamon. From the cinnamon, and the other monastery herbs, the monks make remedial preparations, which they sell in a small store, together with jams and chutneys from the orchard fruits. In the season, they sell cashew wine, which the monks press on site, before adding herbs to turn it into bitters, following a recipe from the alchemist, Paracelsus.

Each of the monks does a share of the manual work, Gabriel says: tending the crops and the gardens, preparing the food and cleaning the communal areas. Mostly they work in silence. The monks strive to live as simply as possible, he says, in harmony with nature.

I spend a week at the monastery, writing in the library in the morning, participating in the daily tasks in the afternoon. The only noise here is the bell, which rings six times a day. There is much that is similar to walking. I get up early, am asleep by nine. Time passes quietly. I have my mission for the day: writing rather than walking. I do no more than write, complete my tasks, eat with the monks, and take a daily walk around the monastery grounds.

Writing makes me look back. I've been on the road a month, including my stop in Kumasi for the Adae. I've come nearly 300 miles. I've spent perhaps 120 hours on my feet. At first I couldn't stomach the forest. My body resisted. I was disorientated. I sweated and vomited. I thought I had a bug, but perhaps it was a different kind of reaction, like the first stage of a cleansing drug. I wanted to give up. My feet bled. I got lost. I kept going. I learned to use my stick to steady me in the mud. I got used to the weight of the pack. I began to wake naturally at first light. I ate simply. I grew accustomed to the rain, to the bugs. Some days I walked from first light to dusk. I felt stronger. In the city, I'd read books that told me to be in nature. I'd romanticised the woods. Slowly, I adjusted to them. My mind cleared. I started to feel the ideas I'd read.

'When you walk for a long time', Frédéric Gros wrote in his book on walking, 'there comes a moment when you no longer know how many hours have passed, or how many more will be needed to get there; you feel on your shoulders the weight of the bare necessities, you tell yourself that's quite enough – that really nothing more is needed to keep body and soul together – and you feel you could carry on like this for days, for centuries.'

Where I'm headed now – out of the forest and into the dry lands towards the Sahel – the distances will be further, the days longer. I feel that with the remoteness, the harsher climate, I'm going deeper, that I can get closer to the feeling Gros is talking about, worn down to the point I need nothing beyond the trail.

# Desert

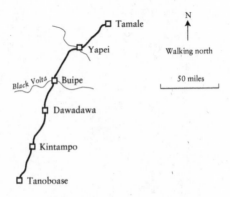

To Tamale, the largest settlement in north Ghana, in
the region of the Dagomba people, home to the shrine of
Afa Kaya. The long, dusty road north from Tano is *150*
miles, passing the Black and White Volta river crossings,
and the villages of Dawadawa, Buipe and Yapei.

# I

It's like crossing the Ohio River to Dixie, the monk said. Ahead, an empty track cuts through the scrub. The sun is still low, and dust filters the light. There are a few thorn trees, some rusted roofs, miles of parched grassland. It looks nothing like America to me, but I think I understand. It's the same country, the monk meant, but I'm coming to a different world.

I'm on the divide between North and South here. At this latitude the wet, green vegetation fades out. The north of the country is the start of dry lands that reach 2,000 miles across the Sahara to the Mediterranean. Northern Ghana is sparsely populated. There's one large town (Tamale). Ashanti influence wanes. A patchwork of smaller-population peoples and cultures resides here, many tied to herding. On almost every index, the north is less developed than the south.

My route north goes to Tamale, 160 miles on the only tar road, the road I'm setting out on now. From Tamale, it's a hundred miles on dirt tracks into the Tong Hills. The endpoint is Tengzug: the tomb of Tonna'ab, the founding ancestor of the Tallensi people. The shrine was once one of the country's most important religious sites and received pilgrims from across West Africa.

The road to Tengzug is more difficult than the one through the forest to Tano. In the far north, my maps don't have the detail to get me all the way. Some days I'll need to walk forty miles by nightfall to reach a place where I can get water. Most nights I'll camp. I need more discipline on this section of the journey: to become less like the office worker I grew into, more like the desert travellers I read of as a child.

The heat is like carrying an extra weight. For long stretches the horizon is empty. Sometimes I pass tracks reaching into the scrub. I make out clusters of huts in the far distance. At one junction there's a picture of a bare-chested man walking through lightning. The words 'Spiritual Help' are written beside an arrow pointing west. For two hours I see nothing but plains of yellowing grass. A film of cloud obscures the sun. The cloud is not thick enough to cool the air. Heat rises from the tar.

At the first village, I stop for water. The huts are made from burnt mud and wattle, some from cattle dung. An old man helps me with the pump. I follow the same routine as usual. I refill my bottles, taking one with additional salt and sugar (which I drain in four gulps). I rest for twenty minutes in the shade of a thorn tree. I pour water over my scarf and wring it out over my head.

Then I go again. I walk for three hours to the next village. During that time the sun shifts barely across the sky. A couple of trucks pass. The ground is dry and unchanging. The heat remains constant.

On 30 December 1935, attempting to break the Paris–Saigon Air Race speed record, Antoine de Saint-Exupéry, known then as 'Saint-Ex', and his co-pilot, André Prévot, came down in the Sahara night, crashing somewhere in the Scetis Desert, Egypt. The pilots stepped from the wreck onto the dunes, with just a Thermos of coffee, a half-pint of wine and a day's supply of water. They spent four days lost in the Egyptian Sahara. As the men neared death, a Bedouin man found them. He administered a rehydration treatment that saved their lives.

*The Little Prince* – Saint-Ex's story of a pilot crashing in the desert and meeting a child from another planet – was the first time I'd pictured a desert. I was perhaps six years old, and I saw the desert then like the Pacific Ocean or the Himalayas: somewhere distant and wild, where explorers went and adventures happened.

Twenty years later, one night at the law firm, I re-read the book. I was working on a transaction which involved perhaps thirty lawyers in different departments. That night was the signing. My job was to type up changes to the finance documents as they came up from the negotiating table floors below, print them, and take the redrafted versions back down.

I'd been working at the firm for three months. I'd heard people speak about all-nighters: they were seen in some ways as a rite of passage. Trainee lawyers spoke of them as unpleasant, but at the same time an element of pride came through the stories: it showed commitment and endurance, and that you were working on significant things.

Negotiations had moved into a second night by the time the directors from the client arrived. The finance documents were in final form by then, my colleague told me, but I should be on hand in case any unexpected changes needed to be made. The businesspeople from the other side were there, with their lawyers, together with all the lawyers from our firm. Everyone had gathered in the largest boardroom, with smaller groups in break-out rooms. I waited in my office on the sixth floor. The bin was filled with drinks cans and food boxes. I hadn't left the building for thirty-six hours and the smell made me nauseous.

Trying to keep awake in case I needed to type up more changes, I googled *The Little Prince*. I re-read the book at my desk. I wondered – as I read about the pilot, stranded beside his plane in the desert, meeting the boy from Asteroid B-612 – how much of the story had come to Saint-Ex as he wandered the dunes, with just his Thermos and his wine, dying of thirst in the sand.

Saint-Ex himself went down a final time in 1944, a year after publishing *The Little Prince*. He took off from Corsica on a bright July morning in a Lockheed P-38. When he didn't return that night, it was presumed he'd been shot down by the Luftwaffe somewhere over the Alps. Six decades later, a diver discovered his plane off the coast of Marseille, hundreds of miles from the Alps. A subsequent investigation concluded that the plane was likely to have hit the water at 500 miles an hour, and, with no bullet holes in the wreckage, that a failure of oxygen supply was a possible explanation for the pilot's apparent loss of control. Others suggested Saint-Ex, who'd struggled with depression, had plunged himself into the sea.

It was after midnight when I finished *The Little Prince* at my desk. I drank another Coke. I woke, hours later, in my suit on the floor, light streaming into the office, having dreamed of thirst in the desert.

2

The soldier at the first checkpoint has a rifle on his knee, a shoot of sugar cane in his mouth. He sits on a plastic chair beneath a tarpaulin. Heat flows from the tar around him.

He asks why I'm out here, alone.

I explain that I stayed the night in the monastery, that I'm walking to Tamale.

Watch for the herders on the road, he says.

I nod, but he sees that I've not understood.

The herders have come south, he says. Do you know what it's like when a thousand cattle pass? They turn the fields to dust. The farmers are helpless. The sticks the herders carry are harder than iron. They're cut from a tree that grows only in Sokoto. The men live their whole lives in the bush. They have no homes, no god, no country.

Flies have settled on both our foreheads. I brush them away, but they seem not to bother the soldier.

The herders will see you and see dollars, he says.

Since I left Kumasi, people have warned me about the Fulani herders who roam north Ghana and much of West Africa at this latitude. As with the Bedouin in Arabia, the Roma in Europe, something about the herders seems to unsettle village people here. They're a sign that I'm nearing the Sahel, the belt of dust savannah at the base of the Sahara.

Now is the hard part of the day. The heat is up and there's still far to go. I have twelve miles to reach Kintampo, where I'll stop for the night. I can't yet say to myself, *You are nearly there: keep going just a little longer*. I have to keep the momentum all the same, knowing it will be four hours or more until I'm off the road.

The land is unchanging: a plane of orange dust and pale trees. The monotony has a certain power. The heat, the dust, the emptiness require a different focus to the forest. I have to concentrate harder. It's a particular kind of endurance.

I imagine myself running a marathon as I walk. This is a daydream I have often when I run. It detaches my mind from any pain or sluggishness that might be spreading through my body. Somehow it brings my head in sync with my feet, so the only thing I'm conscious of is the race I'm running in my mind.

The dream starts with training, months before the race. I picture myself up early at the track, doing my yassos. (These are 800-metre loops running at fast, breathless pace, with a slow recovery loop between each.) I imagine the 800-metre times falling over the training weeks: 3:05, 2:55, 2:45. It's pleasing to feel myself improving, to think that I'm getting closer to my goal.

I work through the race-day routine in detail. I put on my kit, which I've laid out the night before. I eat a bowl of porridge. I prepare a bottle of water with salt and sugar. I pin the race number to my shirt. Then I'm at the start line. I record the time of each kilometre as I run: adding them up is the way I progress mentally through the race. Everything about the daydream is geared towards completing the marathon in under three hours, something I've never managed in life.

Today, I come through the first kilometre in 4 minutes, 5 seconds. This is a good time, on track for my goal. The second kilometre I'm able to hold the same pace. Another 4:05. That takes me to 8:10 for the race so far. I speed up a little, as I'm through the crowds at the start. I make a 4:02. My time is 12:12 as I pass the 3-kilometre marker.

I have to concentrate to remember the cumulative time and distance. If I lose my place the daydream dies, so I focus carefully.

I imagine the determination I'd need at the half-marathon point, how tired I would be, how I'd have to be completely focused on holding the pace. If I let it slip then, all the effort of the training and the race to that point would be lost. I feel happiness as I pass the point – somewhere between 30 and 35 kilometres – where I would be confident that nothing would go wrong, that I would make my goal. For the final phases of the marathon I zoom in, thinking in 500-metre segments, then, as I enter the final kilometre to the finish, in 100-metre segments. I try to stretch out the experience – the feeling of running hard and being nearly at my goal – for as long as I can.

When I begin the daydream, I imagine I might not make it under three hours. But in the end, I always do, sometimes by a large margin, sometimes by a second. I run different versions of the dream each time. Sometimes I let it roll over and over in the same session, moving to different races, progressing through faster and faster times, so that it becomes not a single race, but a longer journey of improving as a runner. At other times I imagine myself at a different level altogether. I'm no longer an amateur, but competing in the London Marathon, running to become a champion. The process of the dream is the same though. I imagine the times I need for each kilometre and I progress through them, doing rolling sums of the time and distance. The arithmetic is why I think the daydream is able to hold my attention for so long. And it's as if the process of running the race in my mind seeps into my legs, releasing extra energy for the slow, hot road at my feet.

3

I've walked for eleven hours by the time I reach Kintampo. Kintampo is a junction town, at the intersection of the north-south Tamale road and the dirt road that runs west to the Black Volta. Trucks bring the only breeze here. A cloud of dust envelops the stalls as each passes. Rotting fruit and flashing toys are laid on cloths along the verge. Children dance to radio static beside the cars.

In archaeology, Kintampo is known for a curious elliptical object, uncovered in dozens of sites in the region, sometimes referred to as the terracotta cigar. Specialists in the region have speculated that such objects, most of which are heavily scored, were used by Stone Age peoples for potting. In the sites in which they've been found, the terracotta cigars were in abundance, suggesting they played a central role in the lives of early Kintampo peoples. Strangely, no artefacts like them have been uncovered anywhere else in the world, and no one is sure what they were used for.

As settlements in the Kintampo region were excavated, a picture emerged of the peoples who lived there thousands of years before. At Ntereso, north of the White Volta, terracotta cattle and lizards were recovered; at Boyase Hill, a clay sculpture of a dog. At other sites, archaeologists uncovered bone harpoons used for fishing, and spearheads of flint and quartz with which Stone Age peoples hunted. Some of these made their way to shrines in the region, where, having been dug up by farmers, they were taken to be thunderbolts thrown to earth by sky gods.

Of most interest to those studying the sites was evidence that the Stone Age communities of Kintampo had farmed the land. Archaeologists found signs of animal husbandry and, in some places, evidence that woodland had been cleared for planting crops, together with indications of pearl-millet and oil-palm cultivation. The early peoples of Kintampo had been, it seemed, West Africa's first farmers.

Where these peoples originated, no one is sure. The terracotta cigars suggest they lived at the end of the last ice age, around 2000 BC. One theory proposes that the Stone Age peoples of Kintampo were climate migrants, fleeing south, from the desiccating Sahara.

The Sahara in the millennium before that time – 4,000 years ago – was in a green spell. Cyclical wobbles in the tilt of the earth, generated by the pull of planets and the moon, cause the earth to face the sun at a slightly different angle for periods. North Africa receives more light during these spells. The light brings monsoons that can last centuries. The rain fills lakes, and animals come to the water. Humans follow the grasses and settle. In what are now among the most arid regions of the Sahara, the dust mountains on the borders of Libya and Egypt, close to where Saint-Ex crashed, there are 10,000-year-old cave paintings of hippopotamus and human figures swimming, suggesting a lush and watery landscape. A short way north, in the Wadi El-Hitan, perfectly preserved skeletons of twenty-foot whales lie in the sands, from the time the Sahara was a sea.

As the earth last tilted again, 4,000 years ago, the light lessened, the rains ceased, and the animals and plants that lived there fled or died. It was in response to this series of events, archaeologists propose, that some of the peoples who had been living on the western side of the then-green Sahara moved to the woodland savannahs around Kintampo.

How they came to be, as far as the available evidence suggests, the first people to settle and farm the land in West Africa, is unclear. At the start of the twentieth century, Raphael Pumpelly, a mining geologist who led explorations across America and Central Asia, proposed the idea that the first bands of humans to stop living nomadically, and settle in groups to farm, did so having travelled to oases in droughts. The archaeologist Gordon Childe popularised the theory twenty years later, focusing on the lands of the Middle Euphrates, where the presence of seeds and fossilised animal dung suggested humans had first settled 12,000 years ago. Childe argued that the density of life found beside the oasis lakes was the catalyst for humans to start farming, as, surrounded by such abundance, they no longer needed to roam in search of game. He saw the moment as a watershed in human history, following which came civilisation, writing, cities, nation-states. Subsequent research has shown that the Middle East at that time did not dry out in the way Childe had assumed, and that the process from nomad to farmer was more gradual, but that the emergence of fertile land in the desert did play a part in driving it.

Surveying the bulls, phallic symbols and mother-goddess figures dug up at Çatalhöyük, Göbekli Tepe and other sites across the old Hittite and Mesopotamian worlds, Jacques Cauvin, a French archaeologist who led digs across the Middle East in the 1960s and 1970s, argued that farming didn't come from changes in climate or ecology, but out of a shift in the human psyche. 'A revolution of symbols', Cauvin said, had taken place during the 10,000 years before Christ, in which humans began to see themselves as distinct from the nature around them. Ideas about gods and human power over nature emerged, which they expressed in the first shrines and art. It was through this shift, Cauvin argued, that people gained the ability to conceive of domesticating wild things.

Kintampo's first farmers feel distant, as I follow the main strip to the market. A line of trucks stands in a cloud of exhaust and dust. I want shade. I take off my pack and lie in the shadows. My head throbs. A young mother holds a boy on the store porch beside me. The boy looks deathly ill. She feeds him Coca-Cola from a glass bottle, cradling his head to force the liquid down. I buy her another Coke and one for myself. I lie back and smoke a cigarette, trying to shut out the noise of the engines.

4

The air is cold in the last moments before dawn. The sky is grey-blue at this time, the moon high and pale. The trucks are silent, the stalls deserted. Dogs move in the dust between the rubbish heaps. They dislodge scraps of plastic, which drift on the road in the breeze. The scraps catch in the thorns. The only noise, beside the plastic flickering in the trees, is the base of my stick on the road.

Dawadawa, the village where I'll spend the night, is twenty-four miles north. It will be four hours before I first break. I think about the break as I walk. Each day I stop at 9 or 10 a.m., before the full heat of the day arrives. I try to stop in a village, but sometimes I sit in the shade of a tree, far from a settlement. I'm happy to have the chance to sit down, to drink something cool. I no longer rush these stops. I know it will be a long day whatever. If there's a village, I refill my bottles and wet my scarf at the pump.

The hottest part of the day lasts four to five hours. Mentally this segment is the hardest. The sun deadens everything. Dust swirls among the huts in the winds. People wait for dusk beneath the trees. The air is still, the only movement the vapour on the tar. I try to shut the heat from my mind.

Each day I've moved north the air has become drier, the sun stronger. The villages are rougher: there's less metal, less cement. The goods in the general stores are plain: piles of muddy vegetables, sacks of grains, cigarettes sold individually. The only things in packets are glucose biscuits.

I find something satisfying in the bareness, the repetition of the days.

Even at home, surrounded by variety, I chose the same thing again and again. If eating by myself, I always bought the same six items from the store: a tin of butter beans, chickpeas, kidney beans, a fresh chilli, tomatoes, spinach. I fried everything together and ate it with toast. I had the leftovers for lunch the next day, sometimes the same meal over and over for a week.

Here, my diet is as simple. I have bread and bananas for breakfast, which I eat as I walk; bread and groundnuts for lunch; and yam or maize with stewed vegetables before I sleep.

I carry few clothes. I have two T-shirts, one pair of shorts, one pair of Lycra undershorts, two pairs of socks and underwear, a linen shirt, one set of trousers and a down jacket. Each night when I get in, I change into my trousers and shirt, and rinse the clothes I've walked in. I have no decisions about what to wear. I enjoy the routine of washing my clothes each night.

The Arabs say *A man can only be free in the desert*. I'd once thought this was about all the space in the desert.

Emptiness can be a form of freedom. Walking now, I think it's about reduction. Conditions in the desert mean you only think of what's in front of you. What happened in the past, worries about the future: these distractions fade out. Everything comes down to a few simple needs. Water. Salt. Shade. Sleep. There's a distance to go, a way to follow, however many steps and hours to cover it. There's no room for anything more. This is a form of freedom.

In the summer of 1895, aged eighteen, Isabelle Eberhardt stood for her portrait in the studio of photographer and family friend, Louis David. She wore Arabic robes, a style she would adopt again and again in subsequent years, cross-dressing, often in a djellaba and fez, as she wandered the deserts and mountains of the western Sahara.

Even as a child, Eberhardt fantasised about North Africa. 'I was already a nomad as a young girl,' she recalled, looking back at her childhood in the villa at Meyrin, beneath the Jura mountains. Her mother was a Russian aristocrat, her father unknown. There were rumours, later, that she was the lovechild of Arthur Rimbaud. More likely her father was her tutor, Alexander Trophimowsky, a Russian-Armenian scholar, said to be an anarchist.

'My soul is in the Orient ... my heart is in Oran ...,' Eberhardt wrote in a poem to her brother, who'd been posted to Algeria with the French Foreign Legion. By then she could speak some Arabic, had read the Koran, and was transfixed with Pierre Loti's novels about the Maghreb.

Eberhardt first travelled to Algeria in May 1897, aged twenty, to the city of Annaba, accompanied by her mother. Her mother converted to Islam in Annaba, a ceremony

Isabelle saw as unnecessary, believing, through her Russian roots, that she had always been a Muslim.

The journey would be the first of many Eberhardt would make into North Africa's deserts. In 1899 she travelled, this time alone, in male Arab dress, from the coast into the Sahara, by train to Batna, by mule to Timgad, and then onto Chegga, where she joined the travelling party of a Tuareg sheikh, before moving further south across gravel and dunes to the oases of Touggourt and El Oued.

What was she looking for, wandering, alone, through the barren Algerian south?

'I long to sleep in the cool, deep silence under the dizzying shower of stars,' she wrote in 1900, 'with nothing but infinite sky for a roof and warm ground for a bed'.

During subsequent journeys, Eberhardt crossed the Kabylie Mountains from Algiers, returning again to El Oued. She wore a red fez and used the name Mahmoud Saadi. She survived an assassination attempt, in which she was bludgeoned with a sword. She smoked hash, drank with legionnaires, gained a reputation for sleeping around which at the time scandalised the local colonial government. The authorities accused her of spying and threatened her deportation. She fell in love and married an Algerian soldier, Slimène Ehnni. She was initiated into the holy Qadrya order at a Sufi lodge. She contracted malaria and, perhaps, syphilis.

'Vagrancy is deliverance,' she wrote in a notebook, a sentence subsequently assigned to her as a mantra, 'and life on the open road is the essence of freedom.' She'd come to the Sahara to escape her civilisation: 'the great fraud of our times', as she described it. The desert was a way out, a place to be free, to plunge into the new worlds of Islam and nomads.

As her relationship with Slimène cooled, and she ran out of money, she retreated to a monastery at Kénadsa, high up on the gravel plateaus of the Algeria-Moroccan border. Even then, as her perspective seemed to clarify, and she wrote of her loneliness, she came back to the freedom she had sought and found, for a time, in the desert: 'Freedom was the only happiness accessible to my nature,' she wrote from the monastery. 'I shall stay a nomad all my life.'

That autumn Eberhardt travelled to Ain Sefra, where Slimène had been stationed. Sick with a fever, she was admitted to the military hospital. Three weeks later, on 21 October 1904, a flash flood flowed through the wadi that ran through town, engulfing the room in which she slept. Isabelle Eberhardt was found under a beam; the pages of her manuscript floating around her body.

She seemed to grow in the years after death. The pages that were gathered from the water were sent to her editor, Victor Barrucand, who pieced them together for publication. Her only novel, *Vagabond*, about a Russian medical student who takes a nomad's path, was first published two decades after she'd died. In Algiers a street was named after her. She became an anti-colonial and feminist hero. Biographies were published in French and English, then novels based on her story. Films, plays and an opera have been produced chronicling her life.

I read accounts by many desert travellers. From all walks of life, it seemed, people who'd rejected their society, had become lost, or – like Eberhardt – wanted to change themselves, gravitated to the desert. It was to the desiccated salt lakes of the Wadi El Natrun that the early Christian mystics travelled; to the dry flats of the Black Rock Desert where the first Burning Man community went to set up camp; and to the desert wildernesses that the elders of many societies still send their young to come of age.

Paul Bowles, who translated some of Eberhardt's writing, and who passed, thirty years after her, the Algerian oases of El Oued and Touggourt, believed there was something in the hush, the endless space, the desert's mineral light, that transformed a person. 'Even memory disappears,' he wrote of the Sahara: 'nothing is left but your own breathing and the sound of your heart beating.' The experience of the desert, Bowles said, could break a person, catalysing what he called 'a process of reintegration'.

5

A woman serves millet porridge from a stove in the shade of a tarpaulin. Outside, children sell charcoal in reworked rice sacks. A lorry has pulled up on the verge. Within the shelter, men in puffer jackets sit on benches around the fire. It looks like a winter soup kitchen, but it must be thirty-five degrees. I take a bowl of porridge. Sweat pours from my forehead as I eat.

Call on Korfi Cru, the trucker in Kintampo said. He would give me somewhere safe to sleep, the trucker told me, whatever I needed in the village.

Korfi lives in a half-built house at the southern edge of Dawadawa. A child shows me to his compound. Two women sit on stools in the yard, loading okra into sacks. Korfi is at the farm, the older woman says, but soon he will return. It will be fine for me to sleep here, she says.

I assemble the tent slowly, working through each piece in my mind before I start. A few children gather, and then more, until perhaps fifty stand in a circle around me. A boy takes the end of the pole, following me as I fix the other end to the hole in the ground sheet. Another child comes forward and takes the end beside him. Then more are there, tugging the groundsheet tight and helping to bend the pole into shape. The children let out a great cheer when the pole clicks to place, and the tent pops into shape. Korfi comes through the crowd and gives me a hug. The trucker called ahead to tell him I was coming, and he calls me 'Mr Robert from Kintampo'.

Korfi's son, Prince, takes me to the pump for water. We cross the main strip, on a path through the huts. It's not all like this, he says, staring at a barefoot child in the dust. Prince is at secondary school in Kintampo, and will soon go to college in Takoradi. From his clothes – clean white trainers, jeans, an earring – he looks already to be there, far from the village. And the way he talks about life in the city, how different the buildings are, the roads, the people, it's as though he's embarrassed about the village, as if he fears I will look down on it.

At the pump, a child finishes filling his bucket, which he struggles to lift. The pump is a regular part of each day for me now. I place each of my bottles under the tap, working the handle gently to try to get the right level of water, as if the water comes with too much force, it will knock over the bottle. I add three drops of metal salts to each bottle, and shake them, so the solution mixes. Sometimes, if I take water from a stream or puddle, I use my scarf to filter the dirt, pulling the cotton over the bottle head, before adding the salts.

As we walk back, Prince asks about the salts. I need to clean the river water, but I don't know if I need the salts for the pump water. I would prefer not to: purifying the water, which everyone drinks, it's as though I think I'm better than everyone else, that I need special water. But now I'm in the habit of doing it, I'd rather not take the risk. I refill my bottles this way a couple of times each day. If I walk a day where I pass no villages or streams, I carry more bottles, sometimes up to six, which adds two or three kilos to my load.

We stop by the ablutions on the way back to the compound. Half a dozen open pits are dug into the earth, in a single, windowless room built from breeze blocks. I squat beside two other men. We each stare silently at the wall.

I rinse my face, arms and legs with water from the bottles. I lay out my wet clothes to dry on the tent roof, then roll out my sleeping mat, and make a pillow from my scarf and spare shirt. I place a bag of food for breakfast – bread and bananas – in the corner, with the other things I'll need for the morning. I pack everything else into my rucksack.

Prince and the younger children sit beside the fire. Korfi's wife works the maize across the yard, pounding the grain with a heavy club. We eat to the static of Korfi's radio and the whispers of the younger children, who stare curiously at me across the flames. It's hard being chief, Korfi says. There are many people in the village, many problems to attend to. In the last drought, herdsmen came south. He gave them land to live on. They never left, he says. Now they are part of the village, but they have a different way of looking at the world. It takes time for them to integrate. Some people in the village said he was wrong to let them here. But where else could they go?

All his older children have left Dawadawa. His eldest daughter is in Takoradi, another is in Kumasi, two are in

Accra. They go for studies or to find work, he says. It makes him sad that they've chosen a new life, so far from the village. But what is there for them here? he asks, looking out beyond the fire.

I call my mother from the tent before I sleep. I have an old Nokia phone, with a local sim: we agreed that I'd make contact once a week, so she would know I was all right. I pretend to myself that I'm making the call for her, in case she's worrying, but really I'm calling to hear someone familiar.

Departing Budapest in 1949, the doctor Edith Bone, then sixty, was detained by Hungarian state police. Suspecting her as a British agent, the Hungarian authorities held Bone without trial for seven years.

The air in her cell was so cold she could see her breath, Bone wrote, and some nights the water that ran from the walls froze. Human and rat excrement littered the floor. Bone lived in the same filthy clothes for weeks. Lack of movement meant she became covered in sores. During one five-month period, she was kept below ground in complete darkness.

Of all the horrors she encountered, her enforced isolation was the most threatening. Loneliness shows up in the brain like physical pain. As with pain or thirst, loneliness is a distress signal. If it becomes chronic, it can be fatal. Somehow over those years, Bone was able to insulate herself from the damaging effects of her isolation, to experience it as solitude.

She created, in her cramped cell, an interior world in which her mind roamed far. She built an abacus by rolling pellets of the black bread she was fed each day. She kept an inventory of all the words she knew in the six languages she spoke. She made mental lists of the birds she could name, the trees, characters in Dostoyevsky and Balzac. She translated poems in her mind. She created challenges into which she poured all her energy. During one period, she focused on removing a nail from the door of her cell, an endeavour that took months. From the towels, which were changed once a fortnight, she extracted the stronger red threads of linen, which she wove, day by day, into a thin strand of rope. With the rope she loosened the nail, wobbling it back and forth, over and over, until she eventually prised it from the door. With the nail, which she sharpened on the cell floor, she burrowed a peep hole in her cell door, using her mouth as a pump to gather the sawdust as she worked, to avoid it settling and arousing suspicion. After months of work, she had a tiny window. When told that she could not have a haircut, Bone tore off her hair strand by strand with her fingers, until, after three weeks, she had the length she desired.

Bone remembered a story from Tolstoy in which a prisoner in solitary confinement occupied his mind by taking imaginary walks. She started to construct walks through the cities she knew, wandering among her favourite landmarks in Paris, Vienna, Heidelberg. One day she decided to walk home to London. She set a distance for each day, keeping record each night of the place she'd reached. She passed in her mind over the Hungarian border, across the Alps, through eastern France to Paris, and north to the Channel. She was never able to imagine the swim, she said, so never made it beyond there, but took the journey in her head to that shore from her cell four times.

I sometimes think of Edith Bone when I'm on the road and I feel the urge to give in: in those moments I'm conscious of my mind pulling me away from where I want it to go, questioning the point of what I'm doing. Then I picture Edith Bone imagining her walk across Europe, how she passed the same amount of time on that mental game, as I will walking a thousand miles of physical ground. Now, though, I think of her by herself for so long, to jolt me from feeling sorry for myself.

As I'm drifting to sleep, my mother calls back. I let her talk, staring through the tent net at the sky. She tells how my aunt has been to stay in Oxford, how she is still volunteering in the Oxfam bookshop – on Friday mornings – and, now the season has started, stewarding at the Globe. They are going together to the bird sanctuary at Orford Ness at the weekend, she says. She tells about a walk she hopes to do over the bank holiday on the Downs, and asks what shoes she should take. She talks about the cases she has at work; how she's been on sidesman's duty at church; how the house is looking chaotic; how a professor from Uzbekistan – a friend of my cousin's – is coming to stay; how she got a postcard from a friend in Paris, who is planning to come to Oxford in the autumn; how they are reading *The Sense of an Ending* in her book group.

I like to hear of these things, to feel the familiarity that comes with the people and places, that life is still the same.

I tell her about Korfi's house, the stew we ate and where I'm sleeping. She's glad I'm with people, she says. She asks me to spell the names of the villages I'll pass in the coming days, and I hear her writing them on her pad. I never ask why she does this. I think it may be so she can look on the map and trace where I am.

6

The herder walks in the dust in the wake of his cattle. His animals are gaunt, with ribs that look like famine, and great, long horns. They move wearily in the heat. As I get closer, I see the herder is young, perhaps no older than fifteen. He carries a flask, a knife and a thin stick. He wears an Arsenal shirt and has a blue cross tattooed on his forehead. He nods as I pass, moving the last of his cattle from the road. I want to stop and share something, to show that we're both out here, together. But we have no language, little in common except that we're both on foot. He pays me no attention and walks on with his animals into the scrub.

In times of hunger, Korfi said, a herder will slit the throat of a cow and drink from its neck, before sewing the wound up and walking on. I wonder if this is for real, or a kind of desert myth, a way to show, viscerally, how cattle are the lifeblood of the Fulani.

In one story about how the Fulani came to be with their cattle, which I found in the monastery library, a man named Ilo, the first of his people, lived in a hut with his wife and a snake, which Ilo kept secret from his wife. One day Ilo's wife discovered the snake, and the animal fled from the compound. Ilo went in search of it. After two days and two nights he found the snake in the floodplain of a great river, surrounded by water cattle. The snake told Ilo to cut a branch from an ebony tree, and that any of the cattle he touched with the stick would follow his people forever. Ilo ran among the herd tapping the animals with the wood. Those he touched followed him from the swamp. The rest descended with the snake into the waters of the river. From that point, the story said, the

Fulani have always carried their sticks, and the cattle have followed the Fulani.

A version of this story appears on the rock walls of the Ajjer Plateau, south Algeria. In those paintings, drawn on the side of the mountains, there are images of cattle, hunters and dancing figures. Amadou Hampâté Bâ, the Malian writer and historian, who was himself from an aristocratic Fulani family, recognised in the paintings, rituals practised by the Fulani as part of the *lotori* ceremony, during which time the Fulani celebrate the coming from the water of the first ox. Bâ saw on the rock walls, robes and headdresses similar to those the Fulani wear today: motifs in jewels; and depictions of the mythical serpent, which the Fulani knew, he said, as the mother of the cows. In the ancient version of the *lotori,* recorded on the rocks at Ajjer, the story of Ilo and the birth of Fulani nomadism was played out, deep in the desert, 6,000 years ago.

Listening to Korfi's stories, I saw in the herders what I hoped for from the desert: hardship, movement, freedom. Western travellers often come to the desert with these ideas. The desert nomad is drawn as the ultimate free spirit.

In one of the monastery library books – *Pastoralists of the West African Savanna* – I found a chapter on the Fulani code of conduct, *laawol pulaaku.* The code governs, the book said, 'the expectations appropriate in a Fulani, a way of life'. The author drew comparison between *pulaaku* and the English-language concept of chivalry. The Fulani code defines, the author said, the ethos of the Fulani, across every sphere of life: how each should interact with strangers and kin, with their responsibilities as herders, and the ways in which one ought to live the Fulani idea of *ndimaaku*, 'being free'. Three core virtues make up the Fulani code, the book said: *hakkiilo*: foresight and common sense; *semteende*: humility; and *munyal*: resilience.

At around the herder's age, the Fulani young pass through an initiation to show they have the resilience to walk with their cattle. Girls who've reached puberty receive facial tattoos, drawn with a needle in dark ink, in a ceremony that can last hours. If the young woman cries during the tattooing, which is said to be excruciating, she has shown that she is not ready, and her passage to motherhood is delayed. Young Fulani men take part in a whipping ceremony, in which each boy whips the bare back of his opponent with a sharpened stick. The goal is not to wince as the stick hits.

I noted down, in the monastery library, the different stories and practices of the Fulani, as if, by compiling them, I could better understand the life of a nomad. I would see, I hoped, that walking in the desert, as I was to do, would require some of the same traits, that it would be – for a time – the same life.

Seeing the boy with the cattle, in the flies and the dust, I feel stupid for the notes I wrote. It's easy to sleep in a bed and revere someone like the herder. Passing him on the road, I see in the second our eyes cross, how little I know of his life. He will likely experience hunger, thirst and violence that I've been sheltered from all my life. His people may die of illnesses that mine are cured from without trouble. The rains could fail, his cattle will perish, and he will face ruin.

But I'm starting to see too the things he has which I lack. He can fend for himself in the land he lives. He's part of a community that retains bonds that have collapsed in mine. He goes everywhere by foot and his body is strong. He has his people's story to give him meaning. He has a clear path ahead of him.

## 7

At midday I stop beside a thorn tree. I've come eighty miles since Tano. I take off my pack and rinse my hands, then my face, with water from a bottle. It's as hot as bathwater. Wiping my face, a residue of dirt and salt marks my scarf. The salt stings my eyes. I shouldn't use the water this way, but it's only a few drops, I tell myself, and for a few seconds it makes me feel a different person. I fold the scarf over my head for shade, and arrange my food. I put a teabag in one of my bottles, with a sachet of sugar. I eat a flatbread and walk on.

Hours later, the sky clouds over. It seems to happen in an instant, and the whole sky is black. The land – orange earth and low green scrub – dulls in the darker light. Dust drifts across the tar. On the outskirts of a village, a man hammers a tarpaulin to the roof. The tarpaulin, held down with tyres and rocks, flickers violently in the wind. A woman sets out pots and buckets around the house to catch the rain. Children peer from the doorway.

I remember a clip about unrest in South Africa on the news before I left. *I just want a plot of land to put my family on*, a man in a worn suit said to the interviewer, standing on a road filled with protestors.

That clip sometimes drifts into my head. I think I remember the man so clearly because what he longed for was so universal; something that should be simple, but feels to me far away.

My mind wanders into daydream as I walk, now through the rain. I'm driving an old car down a track. There are two dogs in the back. I reach a house: on the edge of a village, of grey stone, with outhouses that still need to be restored. The lights are on and the kitchen is full. There are four children. They are still young, covered in paint and mud. There's the same girl I always picture.

I imagine how we built the house from a wreck, living in a van. I took six months off writing to do it. We did as much as we could ourselves, learning as we went, gradually turning somewhere uninhabitable into a home. The house is surrounded by forest. In the garden we dug beds for vegetables.

Each morning, I run with the dogs on the ridge behind the house. I imagine this in different conditions. Some mornings I'm in the rain and the dark, with a headtorch, mud spattered up my calves. Others I'm in the forest as the sun rises. The dogs know the route and run ahead. Home and showered, I picture making porridge for the children, cycling them to school in the village.

Different scenes stream together. It's Saturday and we spend the morning with my neighbour and his kids, working on a fence. I drive out to the far field to meet them, the dogs in the back and my son with me. My neighbour's father, an older man, is there. It's hard work, and we sweat in the sun, as we haul wooden posts from the truck, and beat them into the ground. I feel even through the unreal layer of the daydream the satisfaction of the progress we make: exertion, a feeling of togetherness.

We sit for lunch around a long table in the garden. It's summer, and we have lamb on a barbecue, with squash, carrots and chillies we've grown. We drink and tell stories until the sun starts to fall. The children are content in the garden: no one seems to get tired or wants to break up the gathering.

I imagine the details of the life: the work to upkeep the house; the food we cook; the system we have for the compost heap; chopping wood for the fireplace; the children's bicycles and the stories they tell of school; the decisions we make about pictures, bookcases, upholstering chairs; holidays in cottages on the Welsh coast: sea swims, board games, road-trip storybooks.

Only as the light begins to fade, the air to cool, and my mind turns to where I'll sleep, do I think how absurd it is to be dreaming like this, having run away to walk in the desert.

8

I lie in the half-light a while, pulling my jacket around me. My legs are stiff. Still on my back, I raise my feet and stretch my toes up and out to test my calves. They're painful, but the sensation is somehow pleasant at the same time. As I wake more fully, I feel other pains: sores on my hands and thighs; sunburn on my legs and neck. I reach for the tincture of iodine and douse each sore. As I rub the backs of my legs, my hands collect a residue of dust. These things tell me that I came far yesterday. I walked forty miles and I feel the distance all through my body.

I pack up quickly. I follow the same routine as in Dawadawa. I roll and tie the mat. I bunch the sleeping liner into its sack. I pack the bundle of clothes that I used as a pillow. I shake the ground sheet to clear the dust; put the folded sheet and collapsed tent pole into my rucksack.

I brush my teeth with water from one of the bottles and tape my hands to protect them from the sun. To conserve the water, I rinse the toothbrush with the same mouthful I use to rinse my teeth. I scan the ground to check I've left nothing. There's just the compressed earth where I slept, a pile of branches, gathered for a fire I didn't have the energy to finish. I pull the straps of my pack tight around my chest and waist. I take my stick in one hand and a flat-bread in the other, and walk back to the road.

For a long stretch the only shapes on the flats are the termite mounds. Twice a cattle truck passes. Dust drifts across the sun. I play mind games to keep me moving. Mainly these are breaking the distance and time into chunks; using the prospect of something good at the end of a section as motivation. This makes the distance man-ageable. Some of these breaks I build into each day, no matter how I'm feeling. After four hours, I'll stop. I'll have food, water. At that point I'll usually be a third of the way through the day. I'll do the same at seven hours and again at ten hours.

But if I'm struggling, as I am now, I have to build in more breaks. At the first tree I pass after each hour, I promise myself, I'll stop to take off my pack and stretch. I count down the minutes as the hour approaches, then scan the horizon for a tree with shade. Sometimes I play the same game with herds of cattle or clouds. If a cloud comes across the sun, I pause and splash water on my face.

Today is hard because there are no villages to break in. There are few trees. There are no clouds. I have the blank space of the road, the sun, the motion of my steps.

'Most of the problems in my life', David Foster Wallace said, 'have to do with me confusing what I want and what

I need.' There were rumours Wallace was using heroin. But he could never stick a needle in his arm, he said. His addiction was to television. 'I'll zone out in front of the TV for five or six hours,' he said, 'and then I feel depressed and empty. And I wonder why.' The choice of channels overwhelmed him. He threw out his TV to escape it.

Wallace spoke about his addiction to the writer David Lipsky, who spent a week with him on a reading tour for *Infinite Jest*, researching a piece for *Rolling Stone* magazine. Twelve years later, in September 2008, Wallace hanged himself.

'I may be mentally ill,' Wallace told Lipsky:

> Maybe you're not. But my *guess* is ... that I think a lot of people feel ... overwhelmed by the number of choices they have, and by the number of discrete, different things that come at them ... the number of small, insistent tugs on them, from a number of different systems and directions. Whether that's qualitatively different than the way life was for let's say our parents or our grandparents, I'm not sure. But I sorta think so. At least in terms of the way it feels on your nerve endings.

In a famous experiment in the 1950s, which became a watershed in understanding compulsive behaviours, two researchers planted electrodes in the brains of rats. If the animal pressed a lever, a current passed to the electrode, stimulating the region of the brain in which the electrode was placed.

In one of the rats, the researchers wired the electrode to the nucleus accumbens, a small bulb in the lower brain which it's now known plays a central role in reward processing. This area of the brain 'lights up' when mammals think they're about to experience something pleasurable or discover something new. It's where the neurotransmitter dopamine accumulates. As I light a cigarette, pick up a TV remote, or feel my phone vibrate, it's the build-up of dopamine that I feel as anticipation.

In the experiment, the rat with the electrode in the nucleus accumbens pressed the lever over and over. Rats in subsequent experiments acted the same. All the animals seemed to care about was the lever. Males ignored females on heat to press the lever. Starved rats ignored food to press the lever. The animals crossed electrified wire floors, enduring repeated shocks, to reach the lever. In one experiment, a rat pressed the lever 48,000 times in a twenty-four-hour period, relentlessly stimulating the dopamine pathways in its brain.

I'd read articles on addiction and technology: compulsive tics, dopamine, cortisol. But Wallace had a way of making it relatable. The image I had of him, a great writer, unable to handle the choice that came with the TV remote, somehow made terrifying the idea of dopamine loops, the psychologists' warnings, the electrodes in the rats' brains.

Sweat runs in my eyes. I wipe my face and take a sip of water. At my feet there's a black beetle and a used plastic water sack. The beetle raises its claws to my shadow. I move a few steps on and sit. Vapour rises from the ground. The horizon shimmers. I wait for the dust from the passing truck to settle, then get up. I have eight hours to go.

Being still, quiet, alone with thoughts, walking slowly: these are hard things for anyone. As we crave food, water, companionship, so people crave stimulation. The chemicals in my mind are pulling against the prospect of eight hours walking a straight road in silence. Like the rats, they want distraction, bright lights, new messages, sugar; they want them in comfortable surroundings and plentiful supply. But these are what I'm walking to be away from. In this way the walk is a struggle. It's a battle between the direction the chemicals in my mind are pulling and a slower-burn drive, which drags me on in the hope of breakthrough.

In a cartoon in the *New Yorker* – included on the final page of Barry Schwartz's book, *The Paradox of Choice* – there's an adult fish and a baby fish in a bowl. 'You can be anything you want to be – no limits', the adult fish says in the caption. A goldfish bowl is a symbol of captivity and low horizons. But Schwartz argues that the bowl may be the answer to happiness. 'If you shatter the fishbowl so that everything is possible, you don't have freedom. You have paralysis ... Everybody needs a fishbowl. This one is almost certainly too limited ... But the absence of some metaphorical fishbowl is a recipe for misery and, I suspect, disaster.'

Walking in the desert is a kind of fishbowl. I have two possibilities each day: carrying on or giving up. I have forty things in my pack. I have no choice about what to wear, what to eat, what to drink. The only information flows are physical or relate to orientation. I'm hot, thirsty, tired. I have pain in my feet, a stinging in my eyes. I'm happy to have reached shade, water. The tree is ahead. I've passed the tree. The road is rising. There's a village in the distance. There's a man with cattle in the dust. The air is cooling. The sun is beginning to fall.

I've come ten hours now. As there was no village, I've missed my second break. I'm beginning to reach a place where the battle is not only mental. I'm thirsty, nearly out of water. It's the hottest part of the day, but there's no shade. I feel that I'm sinking. I stare at the ground six feet ahead. The dust is gravelly. There are flecks of quartz and dark rock, but mostly dull orange earth. A trail of black ants crosses the track. God sees everything, Beatrice said in the forest, *even the little black ant on the black rock in the middle of the night*. I stoop down to look at the insects more closely. Some carry squares of vegetation. I fall backwards. The insects stream across the gravel.

Two hours later, I see Yapei in the distance. The river moves with the sluggishness of a body of oil. Corrugated roofs crowd the floodplain. My eyes sting. The tape on my hand has disintegrated: the skin is crimson, the flesh puffy. I try to keep stable as I move. I have a sense that my steps aren't straight. I've come five miles since I began to feel weak. It's taken me nearly three hours. One more mile is nothing, I tell myself. And Yapei is ahead. I see the river, the roofs. The moisture in my mouth has burnt out. My legs shake. I count the steps aloud.

Ahead there are market stalls, a mosque, rubbish crushed into ditches. Men rush towards me with phone cards, sachets of water, fish on rope. Everyone is shouting. I feel relief to have arrived. The feeling comes suddenly and numbs me, as if the blood had drained from my head. My pack feels heavy. My vision goes and I collapse.

I wake on a mat beside the mosque. An old man pours water on my face.

He says I fell.

I look back at the fishermen by the water.

We are far from any town, he says. Where have you come from?

Tanoboase.

He says something to the men around. They shake their heads.

And where will you go now?

Tamale.

Tamale, he says back to me. Do not worry. You will reach it. A truck will pass.

Yes, the men nod, surely a truck will pass.

I sit with my back to the wall and close my eyes. I should move, but I can't motivate myself to stand. It gets dark and I'm in the same spot, on the mat outside the mosque. Sometime later the man calls out. A truck is coming. All around me, men are shouting. Dust drifts across the vehicle lights. I feel myself lifted to the air, laid down.

I notice little of the land on the ride. Twice we slow for cattle, once for a village. On foot each feature would have absorbed me. I'd have noticed what the houses were like, whether there was a pump, a store, what trees there were, how far I'd come. Each of these landmarks would have pulled me forward. I feel regret as we drive, but I had no will left to walk.

## 9

Smoke fills the lanes. There are vats of oil, blocks of shea butter, guinea fowl in crates. Women in veils pass on bicycles. Men usher me through floodlit stalls. The wood-worker has arms like trees and scars across his face. I hand him my stick. He peels back the lead, where the wood has splintered. He saws off the end and bashes on a replacement.

I walk with the stick along the northern road, back to the Institute of Cross-Cultural Studies, where I've taken a bed.

I arrived in the city late. The drive to Tamale was twenty-eight miles and took an hour. The truck dropped me at a filling station by the market. I felt numb then, that the decision to hitch a ride had ruined everything. To that point I'd resisted every urge to take a lift. I thought back to the roughest moments: the storm on the road to Nsawam, throwing up in the forest, walking forty miles in the heat. Each time I didn't give in, I told myself, made me stronger for the next difficult moment. That way, I hoped, I could build the will to keep going for a thousand miles. In Yapei, that collapsed.

I thought about taking a ride back to Yapei, walking the road we drove. I asked at the filling station about a lift. The man shook his head. Nothing was going south till the morning, he said. I gave up.

I walked across town from the market. Travellers could camp in the gardens of the Tamale Institute for three dollars a night, I'd read. An old man in guard's uniform was asleep in a chair at the compound gate. A lady in a nightgown showed me to a room: a monkish cell in a bungalow strip. I hoped to spend a few days, I told her, to get myself back together.

Father Marek, the priest who runs the Institute, is in the garden when I first meet him, inspecting a palm. He has jumping fish on his shirt and a wooden cross around his neck. He pulls a frond towards him, testing the leaf between his thumb and forefinger.

There are more palms than it's possible to name, he says. Hedgehog palms, vampire palms, fishtail palms, bowtie palms, mountain cabbage palms. Over 2,000 types of palm tree, can you believe? We have nothing so exotic here. But we are proud of our jungle.

He lets the leaf go, gently, and continues across the lawn.

Paleobotanists have found fossilised palms in Egypt that grew 30 million years ago, he says. Others discovered in Germany and Svalbard are older still. In Louisiana, the palms are so ancient they've turned to stone. Tens of millions of years ago, the trees collapsed into the swamps. Volcanoes had issued clouds of mineral-rich ash across America, which in time settled, filtering into the mud. Silica from that ash worked its way into the fallen trees, over time spreading through the veins of the wood. The silica crystallised, drying out the woody flesh, and encasing, over millions of years in the mud, minerals of many colours within the ancient trees. The veins of the palms are still visible in patterns within the stones, Father Marek says, which were later used as spearheads by Native Americans, and which can now be bought in gift shops.

The pharaohs packed palm fat into their tombs, alongside gold and gems, but it was a French botanist – Michel Adanson – who was first to classify the oil palm, which grows so abundantly in Ghana. Adanson returned to Paris from Senegal with an oil palm seed in the eighteenth century, including it in a vast body of botanical scholarship – said to have numbered a hundred volumes – through which he proposed a new classification system for the natural world. The Academy in Paris rejected Adanson's work, and he died, destitute. Now he lives on through the mightiest of West Africa's trees: the baobab, whose Latin name, after him, is *Adansonia*.

The first baobab Adanson saw – according to Gerald Wickens' book on the history of the tree – was in 1749 on the Iles de la Madeleine, off the Senegalese coast, and bore an engraving of the coat of arms of the Portuguese king, Henry the Navigator, carved onto it, so speculated the fifteenth-century historian, Gomes Eannes de Azurara, in 1444. From that point, through the fifteenth and sixteenth centuries, the trees feature intermittently in accounts of European explorers, who reported vast, strange-shaped trunks, bearing fruits hitherto unidentified, from the shores of Cape Verde to the banks of the Senegal and Gambia rivers.

In 1592, Wickens wrote, the director of the botanical gardens at Padua, Prospero Alpino, discovered a baobab fruit in the Attarin, Cairo's drug market, suggesting that even then there was some trade in the tree's fruit across the desert, and that its medicinal benefits were beginning to spread beyond the Sahel. Adanson reported wealthy Moroccans, Turks and Egyptians importing the fruit from West Africa. The Ottoman sultan, Suleyman the Magnificent, initiated a custom of giving baobab fruits, according to Wickens, as farewell gifts to ambassadors retiring from Constantinople's court.

Little is known about the trade in baobab across the Sahara, but it's likely that the cargos passed on the backs of camels, up through the Sahel, to the markets of Timbuktu, from where caravans streamed north and east into the desert. Then, Marek says, everything passed through Timbuktu. As far back as the eleventh century, Berber caravans gathered each week on the Niger banks at the settlement, which had grown from nomad camp to city. The caravans brought gold east from the Bambuk Mountains; salt from mines at Taoudenni and Teghaza; copper from the Adrar; and the manuscripts for which the city became famous – documenting early desert medicines, ancient meteor showers, mystical poems and maps of the stars – from madrasas across the Sahara.

I try to imagine, after so many miles of dust, what those who led the first camels across the sands would have felt, as they saw for the first time a palm in the distance. For those travellers – the nomads who forged the first caravan paths across the desert – the feeling of coming upon the oasis, of thirst to be quenched, must have been akin to those at sea seeing, after months adrift, an island on the horizon. Indeed, the wayfinding of desert nomads is not so different from that of early ocean navigators, such as those after whom Wade Davis named his lectures: the Polynesian wayfinders. Before longitude, Davis wrote, the Polynesians navigated hundreds of thousands of miles of the South Pacific, settling the world's most remote islands. European sailors at the time thought the Polynesians must have a secret technology, but Davis, who travelled with a crew on a traditional canoe, tells how a single wayfinder guides the boat, sitting in silence on the stern for up to twenty-two hours at a time. Such is the navigator's attention to the environment that he or she can cross the Pacific guided only by the wind, waves and stars.

Saharan dunes shift like waves, Marek says. Those navigating the caravans read the winds – and from them take bearings – from the ripples left on the surface of the sands. From traces of vegetation they see the history and future of the rains. At night they have the stars. Day and night, they search for palms on the horizon.

A caravan route once ran from Timbuktu to Tamale. The traders were trying to reach the Atlantic, Marek says, to gain control of the coast. But a short way south of Tamale, south of the baobabs, the camels began to die. With the forests, the wetter air, tsetse flies attacked the animals. The camels couldn't survive the illness they contracted through the flies. The line where the camels died eight centuries ago still marks the frontier between North and South. Below it is the world of Christians and farmers; above it: of nomads, Islam and the desert.

The Arabs called this zone Sahel, *the shore*. It has always been the edge. But it wasn't until the eighteenth century, Marek says, when a Dagomba king, Na Zangina, converted the people of Tamale, that Islam settled here. There are many stories about how this came about. One tells how Zangina – then a pagan child with the name Wumbei – was sent to live with the Hausa to the north. The prince learned of Islam, and when he returned to Tamale, he brought with him Hausa clerics, who spread the religion among his people. Another story holds that as a young king, Zangina was losing a war with the Gonja people. Facing defeat, he consulted a travelling cleric, with whom he prayed on the banks of the Oti River. If the king turned to Islam, the cleric said, he would win his war, and Zangina converted his people.

10

It takes a moment to adjust to the light.

Marek had given me Afa Kaya's name, together with a hand-drawn map to his shrine, in Tamale's Kalophin district. Afa Kaya is what people here call a mixer,

Marek said: at once a Muslim cleric and a Dagomba soothsayer.

A poster of Mecca hangs above the television. Beside a tray of liquor bottles, two straw mats lie either side of a board covered in sand. Knives, Korans and perfume bottles surround the board. Candles line the wall.

Afa Kaya takes a seat on one of the mats. He's tall and wears a blue robe, with prayer beads round his neck. He removes his cap and replaces it with a leather blindfold, which he rests on his forehead.

I sometimes passed signs for traditional healers on the road from Accra. Often, the signs listed ailments in which the priest specialised: toothache, impotence, business problems. Some referenced illnesses rarely discussed anymore in the West, such as leprosy or yaws. Many had pictures of a priest in ceremonial dress, photoshopped alongside fire or lightning. I stopped twice to visit temples and receive a consultation. The priests gave me what guidance they could, but I don't think I believed they could help me. I felt like a voyeur, turning something sacred into a Disneyland.

I'd tried to read what I could on West African divination. Most descriptions I saw considered Ifá, the Yoruba religion, the most widely practised of West Africa's divination systems. During an Ifá consultation, a priest throws a divining chain – eight halved palm nuts on a cord – which he or she uses to navigate to a verse of the Odu Ifá, a body of Yoruba spiritual history. The diviner interprets the text of the verse to guide the person seeking help. I liked the idea of those ancient stories, of the ritual of the palm nuts to draw the stories to the present.

In this region of north Ghana, the priests are called *tindana*, guardians of the earth. The *tindana* spend years learning the region's trees and plants. For these priests, as for the apothecaries of sixteenth-century Cairo, the fruits of the baobab are both medicine and sacrament. When a child is weak, one priest told me, they wash the infant in a solution of baobab pulp and cow's milk to help the child grow strong. Though they must take care, the priest said, to ensure none of the liquid splashes onto the child's head, or the head may balloon.

South of here, in the rainforests of central Africa, diviners prescribe the bark of the iboga tree to hunters for stamina and to initiates to trigger visions. German colonists are said to have given the plant to enslaved railroad workers in Cameroon to keep them awake as they laid tracks through the forest. The ceremonial dose is so powerful that the initiate will often not sleep for days. For the Bwiti peoples, for whom the plant is sacred, the shrub transports the taker back to the world of the first ancestors. Iboga, which contains a psychoactive alkaloid that can generate hallucinations, breaks open the head, the Bwiti say.

'[The] road led to a great desert that had no limit,' the Bwiti planter Biyogo Ondo told the anthropologist James Fernandez in 1982, recounting his experience of iboga.

There my father descended before me in the form of a bird ... I saw Christians dressed in animal skins – belts of antelope. They carried heavy crosses around their necks. They were to the left on a path that led off the path we followed. As we returned, my father gave me a *ngombi*, the harp, and he told me that would guarantee me in my life ...

In the ceremony Fernandez attended, the priest administered to a young woman over thirty teaspoons of the bark. Such a dose was required, the priest told Fernandez, 'to swell the soul on the tendons and veins of the body' so the soul could break free and travel the river to the world of the ancestors. As the drug takes effect, Fernandez recounted, the skin starts to feel light like silk, and the initiate vomits, then falls comatose as he or she enters the trance. Fernandez recorded accounts of thirty-eight initiates who told him their iboga visions. Of those, half claimed to see or hear their parents or older ancestors. Many, Fernandez wrote, involved the initiate visualising a journey along a river, path or multicoloured road.

Imagining a walk lights up the same parts of the brain as walking itself. Although scientists don't fully understand why this is the case, research has begun to show deep memory pathways in the brain which activate when walking. Reading the accounts of the iboga initiates, I wondered if this was why so many imagined a path: if it was the imagined steps, paired with the drug, which unlocked the vision of the past.

Aka Kaya has been diviner at the Kalophin shrine for forty years. The shrine is famous throughout Ghana, he says: people come from Bolga, Sunyani, as far even as Kumasi. He helps people understand their problems, to make their troubles go away. If someone is sick, cannot have children, has money troubles, whatever it may be, he shows them how to make things right. Everything comes from the spirits. The way the bones fall, he says, tells him what has been and how to make things well.

He asks that I make an offering and whisper my name into the note. He empties some charms from a cloth bag: tin soldiers, wish bones, palm nuts. He sprays perfume and makes shapes in the sand on the board. He takes four charms and places them beneath a calabash. When he removes the calabash, some charms have stayed upright, others have fallen. He repeats the process three times. Each time the charms fall in different combinations.

My father journeyed to two countries before coming home, he says, pulling down his blindfold. I recently inherited some money: I will waste it. My health is good, he says, my mind strong. But it can be dangerous, what I'm doing. Sometimes I push too hard. I must remember to be patient. The Moon travels slowly around the earth, but it always completes its journey. Remember the Moon. When I try too much, it can hurt me. I would do well to remember that I'm just one person, that I can only do so much. Tomorrow is there ...

... Things will become hard, he says. On this road and future roads. When darkness comes have courage. Remember no storm is so fierce as to drain the coconut's milk. React kindly when troubles come. Ashes fly into the face of the person who throws them. Never be angry. Keep trying, and one day it will happen; things that were wrong will come right ...

He traces his fingers through the sand.

Too often I'm alone, he says. To be alone eats the insides. I must be there for my family. Like a tree, we live to be part of a forest. We cannot do without other voices. I must take time to fulfil my duties, to be part of my people, or I'll find that life has gone, and I will have let the most important thing of all vanish. Only together do we become human: alone, we are animals ...

... I must look for water in my dreams. If I see white cattle, milk, things will come well. I should buy a dove, a calf's leg, seven kola nuts, a can of milk, and go to the river to make the offering ...

Reflecting from his shelter on the Ross Ice Barrier, in which he lived by himself for 150 days of the winter of 1934, the polar aviator, Richard Byrd, said something similar about being alone.

Byrd had travelled to the site, deep in the Antarctic desert, with the purpose of gathering meteorological and astronomical data from the South Pole's interior. In the immediate vicinity of his shelter – which was dug into the snow, and so small he could cross it in just four strides – was his meteorological equipment: a barograph, a set of aluminium wind cups, an anemometer, a weathervane. These, along with the radio antennae and stove pipe which protruded through the ice, were the only signs of human life for a hundred miles.

Byrd slept in a bunk lit by a storm lantern. He stored books, fuel and food in tunnels dug into the snow from his shelter. For drinking water, he cut blocks of ice from the end of the tunnel, which took hours to melt on the stove. Each day he washed a third of his body with the water he could spare. It was so cold – at some points the thermometer showed eighty degrees below zero – that stalagmites formed where the ceiling frost had melted around his lantern. He suffered ice burns if he handled his stove or utensils without gloves. The novocaine in his medical kit froze.

Byrd began each day, waking in a sleeping bag coated in frost, with fifteen minutes of stretches, after which he took breakfast of a pint of tea and a wheat biscuit. He recorded his first weather reading at 8 a.m. Much of the day was filled with keeping his meteorological equipment and the basic components of his shelter in working order. For each maintenance task, he allowed himself an hour each day. When sixty minutes were up, he moved onto the next task. Without such a system to organise his time, he said, he believed his days would feel without purpose, and they, along with him, would break down. He became, he wrote, completely focused each day on improving the efficiency of the task at hand.

As winter drew on, and the point approached at which the sun no longer rose, Byrd described the light draining from the sky, a darkness emerging 'as complete as that of the Pleistocene'. Each day Byrd took a walk in the grey darkness. He carried with him a bundle of bamboo sticks, which he stuck into the snow every thirty yards. Such was the barrenness of that land that if a blizzard came, even if he was only a hundred feet from his shelter, he might never be able to retrace his steps. An identical sameness, he said, reached out in every direction: hundreds of miles to the Rockefeller Mountains to the north, to the Queen Mauds to the south, and to where the ice broke up into the sea 120 miles south at Little America, the nearest human outpost.

Although the ice and the light were the same whichever direction he took, Byrd let his mind wander as he walked, so his steps were transported to the Charles River Esplanade in his hometown of Boston, accompanied by his wife, or back in time with Marco Polo, traversing Polo's journey to China, re-cut over six days and eighteen miles over the ice. Sometimes Byrd imagined himself as an ancient man in the Ice Age as he walked, or watching a future ice age come, the Arctic

spreading before him from New York to California, so
that only the tips of the high mountains protruded from
the white that buried America.

It was during these moments walking, Byrd said, when
he attained his highest mental state. 'The last half of the
walk', he wrote,

> [is] the time when I am most nearly at peace with myself
> and circumstances. Thoughts of life and the nature of
> things flow smoothly, so smoothly and so naturally as to
> create an illusion that one is swimming harmoniously ...
> During this hour I undergo a sort of intellectual levitation.

At times Byrd wrote of almost mystical experiences, of
feeling, alone in the vast white silence, a sense of oneness
with everything around him. 'I was conscious only of a
mind utterly at peace,' he wrote during his first month, of
feeling more alive than at any time in his life. He spoke of
encountering a rhythm, something which communicated
through the silence a connection with the world he'd not
known before.

Within the waves of peace and euphoria, loneliness was
never far from Byrd's mind. When he'd first conceived of
the expedition, solitude had been his primary motivation.
He wanted to taste, he said, solitary quiet long enough to
discover how good it really was. But as the days alone
progressed, his solitude became his greatest fear. If he
dwelt on it, he wrote, let it eat into him, it would be the
end for him. That loneliness was too vast, he said, to face
directly.

In the final months of the expedition, as – then unbe-
known to him – toxic gases seeped from his stove, Byrd

became sick. He became too weak to take his meteorological readings. He was barely able to tap the code messages he radioed to his expedition colleagues at Little America, too worried of endangering them to ask a rescue mission to be mounted. He couldn't keep food down. As it dawned on him that it was the stove poisoning him, he tried to limit its use, lying for hours in his sleeping bag, as the temperature in his shelter plummeted. He resolved then that he was soon to die. In those last days, reflecting on his choice, he wrote that he'd been deluded in what he'd hoped for from his mission. All that mattered, he saw then, were what had been beside him in Boston: his family, and the simple, homely things of that life.

In the final days of June, his colleagues from Little America communicated that they were sending a tractor, which was at that time of year the only way to cross the snow. He received by radio in the intervening days and weeks, updates on their progress. As he thought they might be nearing the shelter, he crawled from his trapdoor and released a flare, which he hoped would light the way for the men who were somewhere in the blizzard. As the flare died, and the darkness closed around him, standing in the cold and the dark of the ice desert, he was sensible, he said, of what he described as the ultimate meaning of loneliness.

It would be another two weeks before the tractor finally emerged through the fog. Although it was two more months after the rescue party arrived before they could make the return journey across the ice to Little America, the presence of the other men meant the ordeal was over, and Byrd began to recover. A person couldn't do without voices and touch, he later said, any more than without phosphorous or calcium, the minerals that make up our bones.

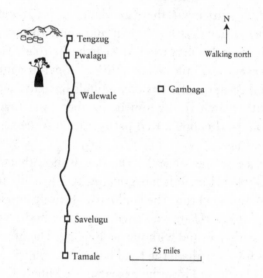

To a shrine in the hills of the Tallensi region, in the far north of Ghana. For much of the twentieth century, the shrine was one of the most important traditional religious sites in Ghana. The road from Tamale is a hundred miles, sealed as far as Pwalugu, then on foot tracks into the hills.

After a week in Tamale, the road is a jolt. It's like diving into cold water. I walk on the verge, adjacent to a black ditch. The first stallholders lay out their cloths. The sun rises huge and blood-orange from the city edge.

The buildings fade to the scrub. On the land at the edge of the settlement, there are dying crops, abandoned dwellings, litter that has blown and come to rest. Then there are just the shea trees, the earth, the road. The villages – every few miles – are a mix of concrete buildings and mud compounds. The compounds have five circular huts with thatch roofs, joined together by a low mud wall. The land is open. Red paths lead into the scrub in all directions.

After a few hours I settle. The sluggishness that was in my legs when I set out has gone away. I get this feeling sometimes when I run. The landscape opens up and I want to run and run. There's no tiredness in my body, and my feet sense the ground without me looking. The process of moving forward along the road becomes euphoric.

In his book on Flow, the psychologist Mihaly Csikszentmihalyi recounts a story told by Tibor Tollas, a poet jailed by the Communist regime in Hungary in the 1950s. To pass the time, Csikszentmihalyi wrote, Tollas and his fellow prisoners held a contest to devise the best translation of an English poem into Hungarian. Deciding which poem to translate took months, Csikszentmihalyi said, as each poem had to be passed, covertly, cell to cell, before a round of votes could take place.

The prisoners eventually selected Walt Whitman's poem, *O Captain! My Captain!* As the prisoners had no paper, Csikszentmihalyi wrote, Tollas smeared a layer of soap onto the soles of his shoes, into which he carved the poem's first lines with a toothpick. Once he'd committed a verse to memory, he passed it down to the next cell, and began the next verse on a fresh layer of soap. For the poem to progress, each prisoner had to remember each verse before it disappeared from the soap on Tollas' shoe. A dozen Hungarian versions of Whitman's poem circulated the cells in this way, Csikszentmihalyi wrote, before the prisoners voted on the winning version, having been engaged in the process for months.

Csikszentmihalyi wrote of other prisoners devising similar mental games. In Lefortovo Prison, Soviet Russia, a fellow prisoner of Alexander Solzhenitsyn reportedly passed his sentence in a focused daydream of a walk across the world. He mapped the world on the floor of his cell, Csikszentmihalyi wrote, travelling a few kilometres each day in his mind, as he made his way on foot across Europe, Asia and America. Edith Bone walked across Europe in her mind from her cell. Christopher Burney, held alone in a Nazi jail outside Paris for 526 days, retraced the walks of his life as he waited.

Prisoners engineer these mental games, Csikszentmihalyi wrote, to give them a goal on which to focus, the pursuit of which can enable a heightened state of consciousness, akin to euphoria, even in the bleakest conditions.

Csikszentmihalyi had himself first encountered this state, which he called Flow and would become the defining idea of his life, while interned in an Italian prisoner-of-war camp during the Second World War. Surrounded by suffering and disruption, Csikszentmihalyi, then aged ten, played chess. 'It didn't bother me that bombs were exploding,' he recalled. 'It was one of the first times I realised you could get taken up in something to the point where everyday life problems disappeared, at least for a time.'

In the 1950s, Csikszentmihalyi emigrated to the States, where he took up a research post at Chicago University. Studying athletes, welders, writers, mathematicians and others, he gathered testimony that helped develop his idea. In moments of heightened creativity, a composer told him, he felt temporarily suspended. A figure skater described it as being on autopilot: 'almost as though you don't have to think, it's like everything goes automatically.' Csikszentmihalyi heard the same from people of all walks of life, he said later in a lecture: 'Dominican monks ... blind nuns ... Himalayan climbers ... Navajo shepherds ...' He came to see Flow, which sportsmen and women would come to know as being in the zone, as the key to creativity and happiness.

During experiments, Csikszentmihalyi gave volunteers pagers that beeped randomly through the day. Each time the pager beeped, he instructed the volunteers to note what they were doing and how happy they felt on a scale of one to seven. Csikszentmihalyi found people happiest when they were doing something that involved deep concentration. They were painting, running, writing, fixing something. They weren't happiest relaxing or watching TV or doing things they thought they craved. They were stretching themselves, in the midst of something hard and absorbing.

'The mystique of rock climbing is climbing,' Csikszentmihalyi wrote of the activity which most often induced Flow in himself:

You get to the top of a rock glad it's over but really wish it would go on forever. The justification of climbing is climbing, like the justification of poetry is writing; you don't conquer anything except things in yourself ... The purpose of the flow is to keep on flowing, not looking for a peak or utopia but staying in the flow. It is not a moving up but a continuous flowing; you move up to keep the flow going. There is no possible reason for climbing except the climbing itself; it is a self-communication.

The settlements thin out. The heads of the paths become fewer. The signs of industrial influence I saw further south – plastic, TV aerials, tinned foods – are absent now. In the villages, children surround me saying *Nah, nah, nah*: Yes, yes, I am fine. They wear torn clothes and laugh at everything. The older children carry younger ones on their backs.

It's a good feeling to take off my pack, to be in the shade. Here, the temperature rises to forty degrees by the middle of the day. Because of the heat, I take more time in the breaks. I no longer feel pressure to make it to any particular place for the night. Because it's cooler, the last hours of the day are a good time to be on the road. I walk until dusk.

Some days I start before first light, at 3.30 or 4 a.m. I pack up my things and walk for two hours in the dark, while it's cool. There are no clouds and no electric light except my head torch, which makes the stars bright. Sometimes trucks pass: I see the light long before the vehicle, but it's still shocking when the truck breaks the silence.

Dawn is a watershed. All the time I'm walking in the dark I'm anticipating the light. The cool hours of the morning are the best of the day. The land looks calm in the dawn light and the temperature is good. But the heat is always coming. For five hours the day heats and heats until it can get no hotter. The hottest time lasts four to five hours. When it starts to cool, I feel relief. I'm nearly ready to rest.

In this way, the days take on rhythm. I have my day-dreams to keep my mind going, and my body is committed to the effort of the road. When everything is in sync, I have a feeling like Csikszentmihalyi wrote of climbing. The purpose is only to keep going.

In his cabin at Walden, Thoreau walked on average four hours a day, a habit he kept most of his adult life. 'The moment my legs begin to move', he said, 'my thoughts begin to flow.' Walking among the birch and the aspen, ruminating on the source of the lake – which had no river or stream to feed it – looking out for eels and mud turtles, he walked into a kind of trance, the ideas for which he would become famous churning with his steps. It was during these walks, which he called saunters, that he conceived his ideas about how to live – 'Spartan-like as to put to rout all that was not life' – and on the deep human need for the natural world – 'The same soil is good for men and for trees.' For Thoreau, walking drew thoughts to the surface.

Exposure to the weather as he walked seemed to electrify him. 'You feel the fertilising influence of the rain in your mind,' he wrote. It was as if being far from the shelters of the social world allowed Thoreau's steps to generate more. Nietzsche experienced something similar with thunder. His biographer recounts how through his early life, Nietzsche had bursts of creativity during electric storms, as if the energy in the air somehow flowed through him, generating hyper episodes at the piano or at his notepads. In his middle years, after he'd resigned his professorship and was working on the ideas for which he would become best known, Nietzsche took to walking for up to ten hours a day on the rock trails of the Upper Engadin and the Jungfrau. Roaming mountain paths, his thoughts seemed to crystallise, sinking or soaring, depending how you see it, into the purpose of life, the death of religion, grasping at the figure he glimpsed in the future: the Being-Beyond-Man. It was while walking a path across the plain at Sils Maria in the summer of 1881, high above the villages of Graubünden, that he came upon the concept of the Eternal Return: the idea – later articulated in *Thus Spoke Zarathustra* – that life might go on and on forever, repeating like an hourglass which never stops turning. He remembered the moment as akin to being struck – induced, he recalled – by the sight of a primordial rock on the shore of the mountain lake. A plaque, memorialising the ideas that came to him there, has since been embedded in the stone. 'Do not believe any idea that was not born in the open air and of free movement,' Nietzsche wrote, shortly before he lost his mind.

Walking a path across a desiccated lakebed in the Mojave Desert, somewhere near Joshua Tree National Park, Rebecca Solnit remembered the feeling of ideas flowing from her steps. What Thoreau found in the forest, Nietzsche in the mountains, came to Solnit in the dusts of the Californian desert. 'To me these big spaces mean freedom,' she wrote, 'freedom for the unconscious activity of the body and the conscious activity of the mind, places where walking hits a steady beat that seems to be the pulse of time itself.'

I reach Pigu two days out of Tamale.

The houses in the village are round with cracked sand walls and straw roofs. Plumes of smoke rise among them. I follow the road to the general store: a mud kiosk with a washed-out Coca-Cola sign. 'Ice Cold Coke Served Here', the sign says.

I want the Coke so much that my mind screens out the surroundings: no power, no fridge, no crates. I point to the sign and make a drinking gesture. When the store lady shakes her head, I yell. *Why is the sign up? Why are there no fridges? It's too hot to live like this. There's too much dust. Why've you not built things better?*

The store lady sits calmly, used perhaps, over generations, to white men shouting for no reason. Another lady comes with water. She hands me a cup and gestures that I sit. The women smile and nod. Ashamed, I offer some biscuits from my rucksack. They shake their heads.

The heat is deadening. I sit with my back to the store wall. There are few people and no cars pass. Flies swarm around me. Gradually children congregate. They peer shyly from the wall. As the group grows, a boy runs up and taps my shoulder. Suddenly there are dozens of children running and laughing.

Among them is a young man, Adupukari. He is the one in the village who speaks English, he says. I follow him through the huts. In the distance, two women haul brushwood from the scrub. Others bring water from the pump. The children trail behind in a great pack, tugging on the straps of my rucksack and pulling at the hairs of my legs.

In a clearing, a group of men sit in the shade, beside a 4x4 that has lost its wheels. Adupukari whispers something to the man at the centre of the circle. The man gestures that I come forward. I stoop and shake his hand. He has a grizzled beard and teeth stained orange with kola nut. Adupukari translates.

The chief is glad I have come, Adupukari says. He welcomes me as his own son. I have travelled far. I will have food, water, shelter. I will stay as long as I need.

The chief crumbles a block of termite mound, scattering chunks to the guinea fowl chicks at his feet. The chicks swarm to devour the insects.

I explain that I hoped to set my tent in the village.

The chief spits a long shoot of kola juice and points to a lamppost at the edge of the clearing. The lamp is powered by the sun, he says. It's the one light in the village. He tells me to put my tent beside it.

At dusk, the men congregate in fresh robes. They kneel to pray on goat hides, reciting the Rak'ah and bowing in unison. Snakeskins hang from the trees. The children sit in a great group around my tent. I sit with my back to the lamp, writing. The lamp gives off a bright white light. It looks to have dropped from another world.

To eat, we sit on a mat outside the chief's compound. A woman with a blue tattoo of a cross on her forehead serves rice and curried beans. We eat with our hands and drink water from metal cups. The men and women eat separately.

How are things in the south of the country? the men ask. They're interested in the physical details: if the roads are tarmac, the houses cement, if there are bridges, electricity, cars; whether people have iPhones. All the money is spent in the south, they say.

The conversation moves from Ghana to other countries. Rashid, one of the chief's sons, asks if it's true that in

jails in America prisoners have their own televisions. Adupukari says this is how it is everywhere in Europe. *Why
would you give a murderer a television?*

In France the government pays people even when they
do no work, a man says. It's nothing compared to Dubai,
says another. The buildings there are tall as mountains.
They've dug new rivers to turn the desert green. They've
filled the sea to create a city.

Europe, Dubai, America are kinds of paradise to the
men, places where everything that's wrong would become
right.

Looking out from London, I saw West Africa in a way
that wasn't so different from how the men see Europe.
I clung to fragments: images and stories that blurred the
reality. From far away West Africa was somewhere dangerous and adventurous. Of all the maps in the Covent
Garden store, it was the place that was the most cut off.
Most wilderness. Most raw. Most likely to make people
go WOAH. And through Vodou, it was the most other-
worldly. I'd see trance dances, ancient medicines, sacrifices. It would be like going back in time. It was somewhere
I could re-make myself.

I never said these things out loud, as I knew they were
motivated by vanity, that they came from the same places
that through the ages seem to have drawn western travellers of a certain type to Africa: dreams of exploration,
Africa as a wild place, somewhere to pit oneself against,
to survive and overcome.

Even in my own mind, I buried these reasons beneath
alternatives: Ben Okri's books, 'the landscape', ancient
mysticism, 'ways of seeing' that have died out where I'm
from. These are half-truths. At home, before I set out, they
worked. But as I've walked, they've not been enough.

They wouldn't stand up when Beatrice or Korfi Cru asked what I'm doing. And the miles I've walked have gradually worn them away, until they've crumbled, leaving bare reasons that are harder to say: I'm afraid of being nothing. I'm trying to become a man. I want to live up to my father, to go beyond him.

The embers of the fire glow in the darkness. The men sit up long after the food is done. I pull my tent behind one of the huts, away from the light. It's cold now. I lie with just the net roof, the hood of my jacket over my head. I can see my breath in the air, stars above.

I read once – in an article on light pollution – that after an earthquake hit the San Fernando Valley, causing city-wide power cuts across Los Angeles, concerned residents called the police. Something was glowing in the sky, the callers said. They were afraid. The glow, the author of the paper wrote, was in fact the Milky Way, visible for the first time with the city lights down. Like many Americans, the callers had never seen it before. They couldn't work out what had happened to the sky.

Anthropologists who study sleep in non-industrial societies have found sleep patterns radically different from those in the industrialised world. When in the early 2010s, American anthropologists surveyed the Hadza (Tanzania), the San (Botswana) and the Tsimané (Bolivia), they found on average people went to sleep three hours after sunset and, in keeping with natural light cycles, woke an hour before dawn. With the exception of the San in summer, no members of the groups slept beyond first light. Two of the three languages had no word for insomnia.

In parts of the United States, sleep therapists have begun prescribing camping to treat insomnia. One study reports how scientists took a group to the Rockies, where participants had no exposure to electric light. After a week, the scientists found the onset of melatonin in the participants occurred an average of two hours earlier than it had previously. Their body clocks had re-aligned to natural light cycles.

I remember the first time I slept in the open. I was five years old. We were staying with my godmother, Lindy, and her husband, Roger, in Teddington. My father had died the year before, and Roger wanted to take my brother and me camping. He'd put up tents in the garden. The normal rules about bedtime, teeth brushing, keeping quiet, were forgotten. We packed sleeping bags and torches. We were in a suburban garden, just twenty feet from the house, but sleeping in a tent outside for the night was then one of the greatest adventures of my life.

Here, there's just the afterglow of the embers; a way off, the lamp. There isn't another electric light for a dozen miles, no streetlights for a hundred miles. The only noise is the murmurings of resting people and livestock. The stars are there. At home, I took not being able to sleep as a sign that something was wrong in my life. Here, at last, I sleep.

13

On the main strip of the village of Gambaga – the dirt road which runs from Wale Wale to the eastern Mamprusi villages – there are soup stalls, *tro-tro* stops, blacksmiths working in one-room sheds. The walls of the buildings – low rise bungalows of whitewashed concrete, and round, mud huts with straw roofs – are coated in red dust. There's no wind. The heat seems stuck.

Father Marek told me about the witch camp at Gambaga. A journalist, Karen Palmer, had written a book about the camp, he said, and had stayed for a time at the Institute. As I make my way to the palace at Gambaga with Mohammed, whom I met at the filling station, I think about one of the stories in the book, the account of Napoa, whom Palmer interviewed here.

Before coming to Gambaga, Palmer wrote, Napoa had lived with her husband and co-wives in a village compound. She spent her days like many of the women in her village: fetching water and brushwood; pounding maize and preparing food; tending her grandchildren and the children of her co-wives. Over the years, Napoa had developed a special bond with the daughter of one of her co-wives, a girl of ten whom, Napoa told Palmer, she loved as her own. At night Napoa experienced strange dreams. She saw herself chopping wood on rocks, Palmer wrote, while vultures dropped carcasses around her. One night her co-wife's daughter appeared in her dream. Napoa dreamed herself as a hawk, the girl as a fowl which the hawk chased and devoured. After the dream, the girl became sick and died. Napoa believed, according to Palmer's account, that she'd killed the girl through her dream.

Arriving at the camp, Napoa would have come to this square, to face the man who sits outside the largest of the palace huts. The man – the chief of Gambaga, known here as the Gambarana – holds a cane and wears a tall hat of green cloth. He's old, and beneath his robes, as he stands to greet us, he moves stiffly. I kneel. The chief places his hand on my head. He tells me not to be afraid. The women can do no harm in his presence, he says. If there was no camp, he says, the women would have no choice but to remain in their villages, and there they would be killed. It's as if he believes the witch camp is an act of humanity.

The same ritual is followed each time a woman arrives at Gambaga. The accused, and those who brought her, come before the Gambarana. The square fills. When the Gambarana has heard both accounts, he takes a chicken, slits its throat, and throws it to the air. If the bird finally comes to die face down, with its beak in the earth, it's taken as a sign from the ancestors that the woman is a witch. She will likely never leave Gambaga.

The first woman I meet, Rahma, arrived at the camp a few weeks ago. Mohammed translates, while our escort, one of the Gambarana's sons, sits beside. A month before she arrived, Rahma says, a child in her village fell ill. When the boy didn't get better, the child's mother said she'd seen in her dreams that she was the one causing the sickness. Her husband came to her hut with other men from the village. They went through her room, throwing her belongings to the floor. They found a beetle. They said she'd trapped the child's soul in the insect, that she was slowly killing him. She'd always been jealous of the other woman, they said. They beat her and brought her here.

Walking through the huts, the camp looks like many villages in northern Ghana: there are mud houses with straw roofs, clothes drying, people pounding maize. Only if you knew would you sense something unusual. There are more elderly people; more people with disabilities; few children; no men.

The Gambarana's son encourages me to take some photographs. I feel like a journalist, and act as if that's what's going on, as if I had the power to share some injustice with the world. But I'm kidding myself. The stories foreigners share are powerless here. A trickle of writers, filmmakers and activists have travelled to Gambaga over the years. The US State Department has formally declared the camp a human rights violation. NGOs have tried to intervene, as has the Ghanaian government, but such institutions have no influence in a place like this.

'Witchcraft belief permeates Ghanaian culture,' the film-maker Yaba Badoe said in an interview about the camp, 'it's part of the ether we breathe.' In the years before the interview, Badoe had made a film about the women of Gambaga. The thing she found hardest to understand, Badoe said, was how the women believed they were witches. 'The more I dug into the story and spoke to the women', she said, 'it was clear that once you are at a camp like Gambaga, just the fact that you are there makes you a witch.'

In a guesthouse on the road south, I met a man called Kwaku, whose story reminded me of what Badoe said. Kwaku was in his early twenties, originally from a village near Dapaong, northern Togo. When I gave him my passport, on arriving at the guesthouse, he said that as a child he'd once seen footage of canal boats in England. Ever since he'd wanted to visit England, he said, so he could see the boats up close. I asked how he'd come to be in Ghana, working in a guesthouse. He told me he was raised a Catholic, but around his twelfth birthday a snake spirit came to him. The snake possessed him for eight years. The spirit came from the sea, he said, and had travelled to him through the blood of his mother, who was from Tsévié, on the coast.

For eight years Kwaku slept in a room filled with statues which the snake instructed him to tend. Each evening he heard chanting. In secret in his room, following the snake, he started to dress up in women's clothes, to experiment with make-up. He felt good during these moments, he said. He saw visions before bad things happened. One day his brother was hit by a car. The snake showed him the body in his dreams the night before the accident. When he woke, he knew his brother had died.

The snake spirit became like a father, he said. He had to ask its permission before doing anything. It was always with him. After a time, he hated it. He couldn't stand the sight of the statues, the smell of palm oil he gave them each night. He went to his grandfather, a priest, and asked his help. His grandfather sent him to Lomé to escape it, but it was no good. Eventually he travelled to Accra, where he went to one of the churches. The pastors helped him, he said. They could see into the past and saw the snake. The snake fled their prayers and slowly he grew well.

Three years later, he moved north from Accra to take the job at the guesthouse. He works hard, he said, twelve hours a day, every day of the week. After a time, he grew lonely. He prayed for someone to share his life with. A girl came to work at the guesthouse bar. He thought he was in love. But he was tricked. The girl fell pregnant. Her sister came to him and told him that if the girl's brother discovered the relationship the brother would kill him. Her bump started to show. Then she cut the baby, he says, and he stopped the relationship.

He spoke to the pastor about what happened, who told him to be patient. Two months after the abortion, a second girl came to work at the guesthouse. They were shy at first, but gradually their confidence grew. When the place was quiet, they sat in the dark under the bar and talked for hours. In the end his prayers were answered. Now she is his wife. He still sees the serpent in his dreams, he said, but it comes less and less.

Kwaku's story was the first time I'd heard someone tell their life story framed through witchcraft. For Kwaku the encounters seemed to have something to do with adolescence, and perhaps sexuality. For the women of Gambaga – many of whom have physical ailments, are childless, or have passed into old age – witchcraft is persecution.

It's hard to know what to make of a place like Gambaga. In her book, Karen Palmer writes that witchcraft beliefs seemed to experience a resurgence in Ghana while the country was under colonial occupation, perhaps as a way for people to feel that they were exerting control, when traditional forms of community relations were lost. For others, it's less nuanced: Gambaga is just an extreme example of men persecuting women. Two centuries after the last slave camps in Ghana were shut down, hundreds of women at Gambaga are held in effective slavery, in the open for anyone to see.

14

Ahead, men drive goats through the rocks. Colourless mountains loom in the distance. Far off there are baobabs. The men call out and I point to the hills. Tengzug is two hours away. The track is pitted with holes. I walk steadily. Now the next waypoint is close, I feel release. It's as though the physical effort of walking, the mental effort of keeping going, are flowing away. My body is ready to rest.

Tengzug was one of the last settlements in what is now Ghana to fall to British rule. In 1911, 260 soldiers of the Gold Coast Regiment marched this road with wheel-mounted machine guns. The soldiers advised the villagers that the shrine was to be shut and the pilgrims must cease.

A similar force returned four years later, but the shrine continued to receive pilgrims. Later, when colonial police were dispatched to arrest the priest, local accounts provide that ants emerged from the dust, gathering so thickly that the whole road was blocked, and the police jeep had no choice but to turn back.

Through the early years of the twentieth century the shrine gained a reputation as a powerful site of healing. In the 1920s, a British anthropologist observed wealthy Ashanti businessmen driving hundreds of miles on the dust road from Kumasi to the shrine. During November, the time of the harvest festival, hundreds of pilgrims journeyed each day from Ga, Ewe and Ashanti communities in the south. Such was the reputation of Tonna'ab – the Tengzug spirit – that people carried mud from Tengzug to sites across Ghana. Believing they were transporting Tengzug's healing power, shrines emerged across the country to Yiehiyi-g, the shadow of Tonna'ab.

I take a stone path from the track at the base of the hills. A child guides me. He jumps freely through the rocks. I struggle to keep pace. We climb for an hour. The huts and boulders below become small. Reaching the lip, the land falls away. At the centre of the valley, a wall of sand rock rings a cluster of huts. A giant baobab stands at the village's western edge.

Tengzug, the boy says.

In the shade of a tree, men play cards on a tombstone. Animal skulls hang above the doorways. A decapitated chicken lies among the cards. The smell of hash mingles with the dead animal.

The men gesture that I sit. A bare-chested man with scars across his cheek hands me a bowl of corn. He asks if I'm an Arab.

Pilgrims come from all places, he says. It's because Tonna'ab helps all humankind.

The man with the scars – Ernest – takes me into the village. The settlement looks to have been carved from the ground. The houses are made from sand rock; the walls smoothed with dust winds. Narrow lanes run between the dwellings, which are numbered with chalk. Pigs and goats are tied to stakes in the open areas. Dogs wander the roofs: they have sores on their backs and prayer beads for collars. Shells and bones decorate rock mounds. Some of the houses are painted with murals of whale and elephant.

I can sleep here, Ernest says, opening a low door. The room has a stone floor, a foam mattress and a leather arm-chair. The room is just high enough to stand in.

Now is the hottest part of the day. Even the children have no energy. The animals lie in the shade. The wind has died completely.

I sit to write in the yard. I have a Dictaphone, which I use sometimes when I walk. I listen back to the record-ings: back to the first checkpoint at Tano; the fumes and dust at Kintampo; camping in Korfi's yard; the road to Yapei; collapsing by the riverbank. The recordings jerk clumsily between these moments. These are the brief interludes when things happened. The feelings welling up in me now are the product of the bits in between, when there's nothing to say: the long stretches walking alone.

I can hear the wind in the background on the Dicta-phone. I rarely noticed it walking. I felt I was surrounded by silence.

'[One] hears nothing, sees nothing,' Saint-Ex said. 'Yet through the silence something throbs and gleams ...'

Jack Kerouac called it the *roaring of the diamond wisdom*: a silence so intense, he said, 'you can hear your own blood roar in your ears ... a great Shhhh reminding you of something you seemed to have forgotten in the stress of your days since birth.' It was this silence Paul Bowles believed could bring about a process of reintegration.

Walking alone and silence go together. But silence is hard. It's strange to play back the recordings. Often, I check in where there's nothing to say. I describe the same thing over and over: the flatness of the land; the surface of the road; the heat; the sky; the time of day; what vehicles or livestock passed; whether there was a village; how many miles I've come since dawn; how many miles there are to go. The recordings remind me of shipping reports from the radio. I guess I found it comforting to say something.

The Arabs say a man can only be free in the desert. This is the Fulani idea of *ndimaaku*. For desert peoples, freedom is roaming wherever one pleases. For me, it became keeping as uninterrupted as possible a cycle of waking, walking, sleeping.

In 2014, psychologists from Virginia University conducted an experiment on students who they asked to sit alone in a room for fifteen minutes, without rising from their chair or falling asleep. The psychologists wanted to understand how humans cope without distraction. Before they began, they gave each participant an electric shock. Most participants said they'd pay to avoid a second shock. But alone on the chair in the empty room, a quarter of the women and two-thirds of the men pressed the button to receive the shock.

Before I left, I pictured myself walking a dust road alone through the desert. I wanted to prove myself. I've realised in the Sahel how hard it is to walk alone. But I think perhaps the most valuable thing about walking here has been learning to be quiet, to get by with little. There was no great danger along the way, no great challenge. It was a slow walk through quiet country. The Fulani say that patience can cook a stone. I think this means that if you have the mental strength to hold out for long enough, anything is possible.

Here, each day is the same: the same wake-up, the same road, the same motion, the same sky, the same twelve hours walking, going along with my thoughts. People adapt to different thresholds of engagement and boredom. When the first televisions were installed in living rooms across America, they were black and white, had twelve-inch screens, and aired three channels. A few years later, at the end of the 1950s, people were beginning to warn that the devices were dangerously absorbing. Now, like the desert wind, people barely notice television in the background.

The last recording on the Dictaphone is from the road out of Wale Wale. It's the same monotonous descriptions: the sun coming up; the road empty; the sky dusky; the land beginning to roll; no cattle; no villages; darkening clouds; six miles behind; twenty-five to go. But listening back, I remember a relief at the sun coming up that brought me close to tears. I remember feeling glad that the land was rolling, as it was something different, and it told me I was closer. I remember the rocks under foot, the energy building, feeling the miles going, jumping easily along the trail, yawning over and over so that I heard a rushing in my ears.

The path to the shrine goes back into the hills. I follow Ernest up the track. It climbs steeply. The sun streams over the hills. Scraps of plastic flicker in the thorns. We climb for fifteen minutes. Where the slope levels, a cave is filled with shattered crockery. A short way on, animal skulls fill another. Men descend past us. Each has a scar across his cheek. Without doctors, Ernest says, people sew herbs into their faces to fight illness.

The path continues along a ledge, to where an overhanging rock blocks the way. Ernest takes off his shirt and shoes. I do the same. We crawl on our knees beneath the rock. The rock sinks to a cave. An old man sits beside a mass of tangled rope. Calabashes, feathers and shells surround the rope.

No one seems sure what to say. Ernest gets to his haunches. The priest looks curiously at us. I hand him a bottle of schnapps. I've carried it since Tamale, so that I'd have something to offer. The priest nods and puts the bottle beside the rope. Normally the spirit receives only blood, Ernest says.

The priest asks why I've come.

I explain that where I'm from it's the custom to travel to sacred places by foot, that the idea is for the walk to be healing. I'd read about Tengzug. The books said people came here on pilgrimage. I was drawn to the idea of walking to a shrine on a mountain in a desert.

When the universe came into being, the priest says, Tonna'ab settled here. The shrine has been here since the beginning of the world. This is why people come. Tonna'ab helps all humankind.

The Fulani say the earth began from a drop of milk: that from that drop God created stone, fire, water, cattle. Ilo ran among the cattle with his stick and the animals followed. The Ashanti call their lands *Amanse*, the Start of Nations. There, a god walked from a lake to form one of the twelve tribes. The Abron story tells how the world began as the children of red earth emerged from the rocks at Tano. They watched as the first waters flowed from the spring to the sea. Most of the stories of creation where I'm from are lost. One from the part of northern France where we went as children says that at the start there was land and sea and no life. A horse grew from the foam of the waves where the land and sea met. The horse washed up on the land. She ate the seeds of a giant oak. Out of the seeds the first people were born.

Deer raised for 1,200 years in safe enclosures still run when played audio of a tiger's roar. Although tigers haven't attacked their species for a thousand years, somewhere, deep in their minds, the deer retain a memory of the danger posed by the roaring animal. I liked reading about the deer and the tiger: it suggests a connection which carries across ages. Coming somewhere like Tengzug, you feel that. Most of the shrines I've passed have been about that connection. It's the same reason people remain fascinated by sites like Lascaux and the Ajjer: it's as if we're reaching back to the most ancient thing we can grasp for help.

Before my grandfather lost his mind, he would sit across from me blindfolded. I sat cross-legged at the foot of his armchair. He had his pipe and his tobacco, a smell of comfort. The dog, a collie called Max which sometimes bit us, lay by the fire. I would tell my grandfather the move I had made, and he would draw down the smoke, tapping the end of his pipe to oxygenate the tobacco, while he ran in his mind the layout of the board. Then he'd instruct me to which square to move his piece.

Sometimes he would play us all, four grandchildren at a time. After he died, and Max went to live with my uncle, and my grandmother was preparing to move into a care home, she sent me a box of my grandfather's chess books. Among the books, which included biographies of grand masters and move-by-move descriptions of notable matches from the early twentieth century, there was a prize from the annual championship of the Lancaster Chess Association. Presented in 1952 by the Association president, Mr Edward Boswell, the prize was made up of a bundle of carefully hand-drawn sheets, each with two sets of pieces drawn on a board, together with a problem to solve. Edward Boswell had included a folded sheet of handwritten notes, containing solutions to each of the problems he'd set, together with explanatory notes. In total there were twenty problems and a dozen sides of notes.

My grandmother told me my grandfather had learned to play chess when he was bedridden as a boy. He had terrible asthma, she said, and in his early teenage years suffered a scarlet fever which nearly killed him. He studied chess books from the local library and played out the moves by himself in his bed, as a way to pass the time.

When the boxes of my grandfather's books arrived at my home, and I thumbed through them, and scanned the notes written by Edward Boswell, I thought how much time it must have taken for my grandfather to get to the level of chess he was at, which was, in the grand scheme of things, still only the level of an accomplished hobbyist.

I thought too about the effort Edward Boswell must have gone to: the organisation of the local competition, and the preparation of the winner's prize, including researching and writing out by hand the pages of notes to the problems from notable historic matches, which arrived, sixty years later, at the doorstep to our house in Oxford. They must have been bored to go to all that effort, I thought then, when I was aged fourteen or fifteen.

What would that teenager have thought about me here, walking months on a dust road to reach a shrine in a hillside cave? Now, when I think of the chess books, and the sheets from the Lancaster Chess Association prize, and I try to picture my grandfather and Edward Boswell, I think that to have gone to all that effort, they must have been very free.

# Mountains

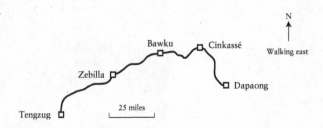

To Dapaong, northern Togo, a town on the borders of
Ghana and Burkina Faso. From Tengzug the road goes
east, a hundred miles on a mix of asphalt and dust, via
the settlements of Zebilla and Bawku, then across the
border to Togo.

# I

The trees have roots knotted like rope and bees in the branches. The tar on the road is wrecked. The trucks cannot pass, and they drive makeshift tracks through the bush. Men with rifles look out from the truck roofs. For long stretches the road passes forest. Mists hang among the hills to the south. Where the trees fall away, all that grows are thorns and anthills. Mountains rise in the distance. The bees swarm around me.

Bawku, the last place on my map before the border, is fifty miles east. My goal is Dassa-Zoumé, in the foothills of the Atakora Mountains, west Benin. Dassa-Zoumé is set on forty-one hills. On some of the hilltops there are shrines to mountain spirits; on others, tombs. In the 1950s a man saw a vision of the Virgin Mary in the rocks. The mountains grew to be a place of pilgrimage. Each August tens of thousands of pilgrims make the journey to Dassa-Zoumé.

I picture Dassa-Zoumé as a mountain village. There are stone huts, mud shrines, firelight. Clouds fill sinks at the base of the hills. Smoke rises from chimneys off stony paths. There are painted figures in the rocks, bones left as offerings. The air is cold enough to see your breath. I've never seen a photo of Dassa-Zoumé. Perhaps it will be nothing like this. But for now, it's what I have in my mind that counts.

I used to dream of my father in the mountains. My father's books filled floor-to-ceiling shelves in the attic, and boxes that had remained unpacked after the move. My brother and I spent hours exploring his things, in the hope we might discover something new about him.

I recreated his worlds in the attic. Among his books were biographies of great mountaineers: Anderl Heckmair, Maurice Herzog, George Mallory. The pictures in the books, which I turned to without reading the words, were similar to photos I'd seen of my father: in the white mountain glare, a pack on his back, rope over his shoulder. My mother had kept some of this equipment: crampons, sunglasses with leather side shields, his ice axe. Sometimes I gathered these items into his rucksack, with other things I imagined essential for a mountaineer: matches, a cooking pot, goggles. I made my way slowly up the stairs with his pack and poles, stopping on the landing to mimic hammering in a clip or to light matches beneath an imaginary stove, which I shielded from the ice winds I visualised blowing around us. As I neared the top of the stairs, I took shelter under the shelves which overhung the staircase, imagining a ledge that protected my father and me from falling stones and ice.

I remember the last time I was in the mountains: crossing the Rozaje Pass in Western Kosovo, following the mountain road over the Montenegrin border, until it disappeared to trail somewhere beyond the Lim River, and then to snow on the high passes of the Albanian Alps. Days after we set off running from Peć, as we ascended through the pine forests around Kolasin, we left piles of sweets and made crude arrows with sticks to signal to those behind which turns to take along the trail. As the path rose higher, we had to scramble, digging ourselves in as best we could to keep our footing in the packed snow. We dipped our faces in icy streams to wash away the sweat. Higher up, as the path disappeared, the only breaks on the horizon were the peaks of granite that rose through the snow in the distance. There, in the deep snow, it was impossible to run. We sank to our hips, stumbling, suddenly far from what we knew, afraid that we'd taken the wrong track, that we wouldn't make it across the plateau by dark. An urgency seeped into us: we fell silent and pushed harder. Hours later, I saw a goat, then a shepherd. That relief, to see another person, and to have passed back to somewhere secure, was overwhelming. We ran towards the shepherd, who moved slowly with her animals into the trees.

For stages of that run I remember feeling so strong I thought I could carry on for as far as the trail would go. That feeling never lasted. The first sign of tiredness came in my stomach. I cramped up, nauseous, and a weariness spread through me. I struggled to eat. My feet no longer picked up the contours of the path, and I stumbled. The miles slowed, and the mountain became something to struggle against. When we made it to Šavnik, five days out of Peć, the two sensations blended, and I felt glad to have passed across the mountains. We were just tourists running a mountain trail, not mountaineers like the people in my father's books, but over that year, when running in the mountains grew to be part of my life, I came closer to understanding what I think drew my father to the mountains. Running a mountain trail, like climbing a rock face, is a struggle. In some way I got addicted to that.

2

A woman in a straw hat sells petrol in glass bottles. She sits on a side of cloth, with bare breasts. Her children run to the road and tug at my arms. Gospel music comes from a church. The men, who rest in the shade, call out in French.

*Bawku, c'est chaud*, the soldier at the checkpoint says. He warns me to take care. I follow the road to the mosque and change the last of my Ghanaian money. Traditionally Muslims haven't been able to own land here, and over time they've come to control other assets of value: cattle and cash. Bullet holes mark the mosque walls. Years ago, there was a dispute over who would be chief in Bawku. When fighting broke out, the government deployed the army. The dispute never fully went away. This is the reason for the soldier's warning.

I lay out the map of Togo on the floor before I sleep. At home, I'd circled the villages where I thought I'd spend the night, noting the distances between. There's one road south through northern Togo. It starts at Cinkassé, the first town across the border, and goes 150 miles to Kara, the largest settlement in the north of the country. The road crosses dry savannah and low hills, it said in my guidebook. I trace the road with my finger, saying aloud the names of the villages I'll pass, practising my French.

The story of Togo, my guidebook said, begins with a Portuguese ship landing in the fifteenth century. The two explorers who led the expedition, Pêro Escobar and João de Santarém – part of the same wave of Portuguese sailors who engraved the coat of arms on the baobab on the Iles de la Madeleine – are credited as the first Europeans to set foot in what is now Togo. I struggled to find information about the country before this moment. It may be that few things before this time were written down, or that people just aren't interested in this period. It seemed odd, though, for the history of a place to begin with the arrival of a foreign ship 500 years ago.

The sailors planted giant crucifixes on the beaches where they landed. They broke up rocks to build their chapel, at what became the Castle of St George of the Mine, at Elmina. Stones are sacred here and, as the sailors smashed the boulders, fighting broke out with local people. The settlers prevailed, and completed the chapel, which they consecrated to Saint George. Every Sunday, the congregation prayed for the soul of Henry the Navigator and for the dead members of the Order of the Knights of Christ.

The fort at Elmina, and others the Portuguese built along the coast, such as the Fort of St John the Baptist, at Ouidah, went on to become some of the largest slave ports in West Africa. Fuelled by demand for slaves by the British, Portuguese, French and Dutch, wars broke out across West Africa. Togo lay between the powerful states of Ashanti in the west, and Dahomey and Oyo in the east. Raiding parties from these states brought prisoners of war, refugees and captives from villages to sell in the coastal markets that grew beside the old Portuguese forts. No records were kept of how many were killed in these wars, nor how many died in transit, but historians estimate that millions perished before they even reached the markets on the coast.

Communities from across Togo – Aja, Ewe, Mina – were decimated. Although there's insufficient evidence to say how many people from each region were taken, documents from arrival points in America suggest that the Gbe-speaking peoples of Togo and Benin, alongside the Kongo of Angola and the Mandé of Guinea, were the highest numbers of any peoples enslaved during the Atlantic trade.

In 1884, just three decades after slavery had finally been made illegal in Dahomey, the SMS *Sophie*, a steam corvette built three years earlier for the German navy at Gdańsk, docked on the Togolese coast. It was one of hundreds of European ships landing across Africa at that time. By the start of the twentieth century, 90 per cent of the continent had been taken as colonies. German soldiers marched from the SMS *Sophie* to Anécho – a village made infamous as a slave port under its old name of Little Popo – and brought back to the boat a group of Ewe chiefs. Left with no alternative, the chiefs signed a treaty recognising German control over their lands. The Germans sent more ships and more men, and moved further north, often under the pretext of scientific exploration, forcing local chiefs to sign away more and more of their land until, by the end of the century, the German colony of Togoland extended over what is now Togo and much of the Volta Delta of eastern Ghana.

German rule in Togoland collapsed soon after the outbreak of the First World War. Allied naval forces cut the German sea cables that ran from Monrovia, now the Liberian capital, to Tenerife, which gave the colonial government of Togoland a line of communication to Berlin and the German navy. Stranded between Togo's mountains to the north, French Dahomey to the east and the

British Gold Coast to the west, with a single telegraph station to get messages out of the country, and just a small force of 700 *Schutztruppe* – German colonial corps – for protection, the acting governor, Georg von Döring, sent a message to the Gold Coast government proposing Togoland remain neutral through the war, and retreated to Kamina, where the last telegraph station in the country stood. Döring's proposal was rejected. The British invaded at Lomé; the French from Dahomey. It was reported that as the Germans retreated, local people set fire to colonial government buildings.

The borders drawn up by the British and French at Versailles in 1919, which had divided German Togoland in half, brought newly independent Togo and Ghana to the brink of war in the 1960s. The European powers had cut in two the homeland of the Ewe people, who lived in large numbers in the Eastern Volta and Togo's south-west. The young governments of Togo and Ghana both proposed the split half come within their borders.

Such was the tension over the issue that, when the body of Togo's first president, the freedom fighter Sylvanus Olympio, was discovered at dawn on 13 January 1963 at the gates of the US embassy by the American ambassador, some in Togo accused Ghana of involvement in his assassination. It was only years later, when Gnassingbé Eyadéma – who became president of Togo in 1967 and ruled the country for thirty-seven years – claimed that he had fired the bullet that killed Olympio, that it became clear who was behind the coup.

Eyadéma's rule was filled with terrible stories. When he emerged unharmed from a plane crash in the 1970s, he presented his escape as messianic, saying he'd walked unburnt from the flames, when all other passengers had perished. The stories of his cult, many of which became lost in myth, were occasionally gathered in the op-eds of American newspapers, presenting him as the most terrible of the world's dictators. Eyadéma reportedly travelled with a troupe of a thousand dancers who sang his name; commissioned a comic that presented him as superhuman; distributed wristwatches to villagers on which his portrait was printed. All the while, he oversaw the killing of thousands of dissidents, and Togo remained one of the world's poorest countries. Eyadéma died in 2005 – then the longest-serving leader in Africa – and his son, Faure Gnassingbé, took power. Faure Gnassingbé is president still.

These changes in governments, the invasions and revolutions, and the events and places that populate Togo's history books, happen in the south of the country, beyond the Atakora Mountains. Togo's north, in the pages of the books, appears like the time before the Portuguese ships: blank.

I leave Bawku at first light. It has rained overnight and tadpoles swim in puddles on the track. Children walk to the fields with machetes. At the fork in the road, I ask the men beneath the tree how far to Cinkassé. Forty kilometres, the first man says. The second says I must follow the powerlines: it's three hours this way. The last says the river is in flood. The road will be impassable. I will have to swim.

I feel that I've been circling the same tracks, the same trees, for hours. Dragonflies hover around my head, dropping suddenly, then rising so I feel them at the corner of my eye. Stubble crops grow in the orange earth. Where there are trees, they overhang the track, leaves full from the night's rain. The sight of the border – a lone bungalow in a dust clearing – is a relief. There's little here. Plastic bags drift through the dust. Men with scooters wait. A guard chews cane.

In the town of Cinkassé, bamboo stakes prop up power lines and barbed wire runs along the roofs. Veiled women sit with bottles of gasoline. Burning rubbish fills the gutters. Men walk donkeys through the dust, weighed down with cloth and plantains. The herders lean on their sticks, rifles slung across their shoulders.

A soldier draws up beside me. He tells me to get on his scooter. We burn through dust alleys, children and livestock scattering, the light fading. The soldier stops outside a building on a narrow street. He bangs a metal door. An old man with a candle pulls back a lock. The soldier nods. I follow the man up the stairs, along an unlit corridor.

The room is furnished with a foam mattress, a mirror and a bucket. I resist the urge to lie down. I stare for a moment at the mirror, holding the candle close to the glass. I haven't seen my reflection for weeks. My beard has grown thick. The skin around it is coated in dust and streaked with salt. My eyes are gaunt, my arms thin. I thought the journey would make me look strong, but I'm worn down. I take off my scarf, then my shirt and shorts. The sun and dust have turned my neck and lower arms dark. My shorts have squashed the hairs on my upper legs, and there are sores on my thighs where the skin has chaffed. Red lines run across my shoulders where the pack has dug in. The fat on my belly has gone, and stretch marks run up my torso. My ribs jut out above my stomach. The journey has stripped me bare. I look wasted.

### 3

At each village on the road to Dapaong I stop to douse my scarf at the pump. By the time the heat has come fully, late in the morning, I'm on a long, dust stretch where there are no houses or crops. I pass a dead cow. The animal has a swollen stomach, legs rigid in the air. The flies rise. I gag, pulling my scarf across my face.

I feel that I'm losing power as I walk. In the near distance there are plains of red earth, villages of mud huts and straw roofs. But the shade is far. I turn from the road and lie beside a stream. I roll onto my side. Three trucks pass in quick succession. My stomach tightens. I try to throw up, but nothing comes. A woman walks by, gold hanging from her ears, blue tattoos etched across her face. She stares from beneath her veil. I feel the sweat running in my eyes. I shit uncontrollably over the dust beside the rocks.

I get up slowly, resting heavily on my stick. All the things I want – somewhere to lie down, water, shelter from the sun – are far. Getting up takes great effort. I remember the river in Yapei, the old man pouring water on my face. I remember the numbness watching the land pass in the truck. Each time I didn't give up, I told myself, would make me stronger for the next day. That way I'd build the will to carry on for a thousand miles. I grip my stick like a lame man. I let the effort of each step absorb me. I try to shut out the land, the wind, the cramps in my belly.

I walk for an hour. Normally I measure distance by my steps. I know that each twenty minutes I walk is a mile. But when I slow right down, as I am now, this system collapses. I've lost any sense of how far I've come, and I have no sense of how far there is to go. Each time I stop, it's harder to get up. The consequences of not moving are bad. I'm only partly in the shade. If I don't get up, I'll be out here through the night. I have no food, no fresh water. I look at the ants on the orange earth, the patch of diarrhoea a few feet away. Perhaps out of an unconscious urge to do something, I make shapes with my hands in the dust. I think of the story of the leopard and the tortoise.

The leopard has been hunting the tortoise for a long time without success, the elder said to his people. When at last the leopard comes across the tortoise on a deserted road, the tortoise asks for a moment to reflect before his death. The leopard grants the tortoise his wish. But instead of sitting quietly, the tortoise scratches furiously at the earth, throwing mounds of sand to the air, so all around the land is disturbed. The leopard asks what the tortoise is doing. 'I'm doing this because when I'm dead,' the tortoise says, 'I want anybody who passes by this place to stop and say, "Two people struggled here. A man met his match."'

In *Anthills of the Savannah*, the book in which the story appears, the fable is an allegory for the struggle of a repressed people. But when Chinua Achebe, who wrote it, has subsequently been asked for his opinion on the meaning of life, he has told the story of the leopard and the tortoise. The lesson, he says, is that struggle is what gives life meaning. And the story of the struggle has to be told. For Achebe, these things – struggle and story – are the two elements of what it means to be alive.

I force myself up, rolling first to my front, then to my knees. As the wind blows, dust swirls around me. I pull my scarf across my face. The wind seems to intensify the heat.

During the Harmattan, which occurs here from late November to March, dust hangs over the skies of northern Togo. The Harmattan winds gather sediments from the low basins of the eastern and central Sahara, carrying dusts west which can obscure the sun for days. When the Harmattan is bad, planes cannot take off or land. The air is so dry trees crack open. People's faces are grey with dust and their noses bleed.

The winds carry the dusts far. High in the Jungfrau region of the Bernese Alps, close to the Mönchsjoch cabin, bacteria have been found trapped in the snow, living on Saharan dust particles. The bacteria had survived a journey on the winds of a thousand miles, and somehow came to rest in the Alpine ice, 3,000 metres up. Atmospheric scientists have found Saharan sediments as far as the Amazon rainforests and the Caribbean Sea. Composed of the remains of Saharan microorganisms, the Harmattan dusts are dense in phosphorous, which enriches the Amazon soils.

North into Algeria, the dust winds have shaped mountains. The vermilion rocks of the Ajjer and the Hoggar ranges, cut first by ancient rivers, have since been carved and smoothed by the winds, which have blown them into a strange landscape of tors and chasms. It was to these mountains, in October 1901, that the French priest Charles de Foucauld travelled from Béni Abbès, an oasis in the Saoura Valley, then on, up through the high passes of the Hoggar, to the plateau at Assekrem. At close to

10,000 feet, on a flat ridge of dust rock overlooking the desert, de Foucauld set to work on his hermitage, bringing mud and stone by camel up the steep mountain tracks. If you see a photo of de Foucauld's hut, in the pale blue sky, the glare so bright it turns the rock white, you might believe you were staring at an Arctic research shelter. One might wonder, too, what other purpose there could be for a building somewhere so desolate.

De Foucauld had travelled first to North Africa, deserting life as a cavalry officer in the French army, with the goal of forming a brotherhood with whom he could live among and pray. When no one joined him, he travelled into the mountains, to Tamanrasset. He lived during those years among the Tuareg, learning their language, and administering, where he was able, to the medical needs of the community of which he became part. He retreated finally to the plateau at Assekrem, where, in 1916, five years after completing his hut, he was killed by Bedouin raiders. A century on from de Foucauld's death, a small number of monks still occupy his Hoggar Mountain hermitage, the roof of which has since been painted with the symbol of de Foucauld's brotherhood: a crucifix rising from a red heart.

The same symbol is painted on a stained-glass window set into the wall of a sandstone chapel, consecrated to de Foucauld, in the mountain monastery of Notre Dame de l'Atlas, a thousand miles north in Morocco. Some among the seven monks who live and tend the monastery – the grounds of which smell, depending on the winds, of the pines which rise above the monastery walls, or the apple orchards which grow across that plateau – migrated to the site from the abbey of Tibhirine, in the foothills of the Tell Atlas Mountains, outside the Algerian town of Médéa. It was at Tibhirine, on the night of 26 March 1996 – three hours before the monks were to begin the first vigil of the day – that seven of the monks were kidnapped. Their bodies were found two months later, beheaded.

At ten each morning at Notre Dame de l'Atlas, Jean-Pierre Schumacher, one of two monks who survived the Tibhirine attack, gathers in a small outhouse with the other monks, monastery workers and any guests who happen to be staying in the cells reserved for travellers. He shares with those present a baguette with tinned fish and mint tea. In winter – when snow coats the monastery grounds – the monks wear layers and layers of robes, each as heavy as a blanket, to keep from freezing in that out-house, the chapel, or their cells, in which no fires warm the icy mountain air.

It's not clear if any of de Foucauld's followers were present at Assekrem on 1 May 1962, when, a hundred kilometres north of the hermitage, a nuclear bomb exploded, releasing a plume of rock and dust from the mountains. The bomb was one of thirteen the French detonated in the early 1960s – each codenamed after a precious stone – in tunnels dug into the rock close to In-Ekker, a village on the edge of the Hoggar. In the test that took place on 1 May, named after the rock crystal, beryl, measures put in place to contain the nuclear fall-out failed, and radioactive dusts rose into the sky. Soon after the explosion, the wind changed direction, blowing the toxic cloud towards a crowd of military and civilian onlookers, which included the French Defence Minister, Pierre Messmer, and the Minister for Scientific Research, Gaston Palewski.

A subsequent report, published by the International Atomic Energy Agency in 2005, concluded that, with the exception of one site at Reggane, a second test region in the Algerian Sahara, and the area in the immediate vicinity of the tunnel in which the failed containment of the Beryl bomb occurred, the land around the sites appeared free of residual radioactive material. The Atomic Agency mission noted, however, that there were potential risks to nomadic herders, as, if their livestock were to graze the sparse vegetation that grows on the slopes around In-Ekker, and the animals swallowed radionuclides that had been drawn up by the plants or deposited in radioactive dust on the leaves, the herders could ingest the same radioactive material through the milk of their animals. It was important, the authors of the report concluded, that fencing built to shut off the site in the 1960s be strengthened, and signs be updated to clearly communicate the dangers of the area to any passing nomad.

I thought then about the only nomadic peoples I'd encountered before my walk, a Khoisan group in the Kalahari region of southern Africa. The Khoisan are one of the few peoples who continue to practise persistence hunting: a technique through which the hunters, traditionally in small bands, track an animal on foot, using spoor and footprints to keep close, until the creature reaches the limit of its endurance and, able to go no further, collapses. Louis Liebenberg, who in the 1980s and 1990s accompanied Khoisan groups hunting, and has since argued that tracking is the origin of science, recorded the details of several hunts in which he participated, including the prey hunted, the distance covered and the speed at which the hunters ran. The hunters in Liebenberg's paper, who stopped regularly to retrace the animal's trail, ran on average between thirty and forty kilometres before making their kill, moving at a speed of between six and ten kilometres per hour. On most of the hunts recorded by Liebenberg, the hunters began in the middle of the day, when temperatures ranged between thirty-nine and forty-two degrees.

I try to imagine that heat. It's hard to think of the air being hotter, but here it can only be thirty-five or thirty-six degrees. I've come today a similar distance to the hunters Liebenberg accompanied. At this stage they would be kneeling over their prey. They'd have no water, no shelter, still to carry the body back to the group. In a sense there would be no end point for them: each day they would be moving again, and another hunt would soon begin.

For those who practise a traditional Khoisan way of life, the pounding of the hunters' footsteps is like a pulse. The beat starts before an infant can walk – each year Khoisan mothers are estimated to carry their babies 1,500 miles on foot – and lasts to the final days of life. Among certain Khoisan peoples, when an elder has become too weak to walk with the band, their people build him or her a simple shelter from branches. They provide them with a small supply of food and light a fire – *to light their way to the next world*, Wade Davis wrote – before walking on, leaving the old person, who at last can walk no further, to waste into the ground or be eaten. It's as if, for those Khoisan, walking is the beat of life itself.

Visiting my grandmother, soon after she'd been admitted to a care home in Westerham, Kent, I thought the Khoisan way might be more humane than the end she faced, surrounded by carers, on a chair in a heated room.

When my grandmother had passed the point where she could recognise us, and she called me by my father's name, or just stared at us blankly, her carers wheeled her to the dayroom window. She spent the last days until her death there, as, her carers said, she liked to watch the squirrels on the lawn. Now, as the sun starts to fall, I wonder about the two ends, and I think how fearful I would be on my own in the desert in the shelter of the branches.

The fading light jolts me. I suck the final drops of water from my bottle and roll to my feet, taking care to avoid the crusts of excrement that have dried in the dirt. The wind has died, the dust settled. I process little of the final hours to Dapaong. I don't have the energy to find my head torch, so I walk semi-blindly through the dusk. I hold my stick in my right hand, and hook my left beneath the strap of my pack. I try to stay on the narrow lane of earth between the tar and the ditch, but sometimes I stray into the road, or down into the ditch.

I collapse at the edge of Dapaong. Opening my eyes, I roll to my side. There are fires across the street and lights in some of the stores. Children wait with rickshaws. The children form a circle around me. When I sit up, they pull back, as if they'd startled a wounded animal. I try to smile. A girl points to my face. I put my hand to my cheek, feel a film of watery blood on my fingers. Someone lifts me onto a scooter. I hold the driver's waist, concentrating to keep my leg from the exhaust. A second scooter follows with my pack and stick. At the end of a dust road, a man in a shirt and tie stands at the hotel gate, under a light, beside a wooden elephant. The men take an arm each and help me to a room.

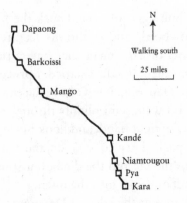

*To Kara, a town in the Kabye Hills. South from
Dapaong through the remote north of Togo. The road
goes from the southern edge of the Sahel, 150 miles,
towards the Atakora Mountains, via the settlements of
Mango, Kandé and Niamtougou.*

4

The doctor says he was trained in China, as if I might doubt him otherwise. He raises the lids of my eyes and says something I don't understand. He makes me drink salts and writes a list of medicine for me to buy. I leave the hotel compound once to buy medicine and oranges. The days blur. I sleep while it's light; eat barely; spend the nights staring at the fan. Each night I take supper in the hotel restaurant. The news crackles from a black-and-white screen, interrupted by occasional blackouts: *coup d'état en Egypte, état d'urgence au Mali, crise humanitaire en Syrie*. Each night the waiter brings tea and asks of my condition. With the exception of two American missionaries, stopping a night on the way south, I'm the only guest.

You can come home any time, my mother says each time we speak. Each morning I lie in the netting, waiting for light to seep into the room. I sit for the first minutes of the day beneath the tap that comes from the bathroom wall, watching the sky go grey to orange through the gauze, hoping the jet of cold will fix me.

Vincenz Priessnitz, from his spa at Graefenberg, in the mountains of Austrian Silesia, was said to make his patients stand beneath jets of ice water so strong they knocked grown men to the floor. He'd first begun to experiment with cold water, according to his 1843 treatise on the therapy, after observing a lame deer approach a mountain stream and bathe a wounded limb in the icy water. Priessnitz saw, so the account says, the deer return at the same time each day for two weeks, emerging from the water each time with a reduced limp, until the creature appeared to have healed completely. Accounts of

Priessnitz's subsequent epiphany differ. In some texts it's said he was hauling wood in a snowstorm, when the bolt failed on a loaded cart, and he was crushed. In a biography written by one of his patients, Captain Richard Claridge, the same injury – crushed ribs, which doctors at the time said would leave him forever crippled – were attributed instead to a cart horse, said to have kicked Priessnitz in the chest. Whichever occurred, the stories provide that on regaining consciousness, Priessnitz remembered the deer from years before, and set about trying to heal himself in the local streams.

Hearing stories of his swift recovery, those with ailments from surrounding villages travelled to the Priessnitz farmstead. Priessnitz instructed those who came to bathe in the ice streams that ran through the forests above the village. Stories of miraculous healing spread. By 1842, according to Claridge's biography, Priessnitz had converted the farm to a spa, complete with beds for 200 patients, communal areas for dining, and a bath with a circumference of thirty feet, fed with mountain water via pipes from the slopes above.

Patients travelled, according to Claridge, with ailments as diverse as gout, scrofula, syphilis, rheumatism, insomnia and mental instability. By Priessnitz's own account, he healed no fewer than 7,000 patients, who often stayed at Graefenberg for months, and to whom he prescribed a strict regime of cold water bathing, a light diet and mountain walks. Patients came from as far as Russia, Brunswick and the Duchy of Baden. On the track from Jesenik to the village, some of those who'd made the pilgrimage to Graefenberg erected monuments to Priessnitz. *Au génie de l'eau froide*, read the plaque beneath the fountain built by those who'd travelled from Moldavia and Wallachia. A statue of a lion was constructed a short way up the road, under which a group of Hungarians thanked Preissnitz for causing the virtues of cold water to again be known. In three months under the care of Priessnitz, Captain Claridge claimed to have drunk 1,500 tumblers of water, perspired for 200 hours, walked 1,000 miles and taken 900 cold baths.

In his biography, Claridge traced the history of cold-water bathing back to those he saw as the fathers of civilisation. Spartan warriors bathed daily in the cold waters of the Eurotas, he wrote, to strengthen their bones. Hippocrates recommended spring water to fight sickness; Pythagoras to keep strong. Girolamo Savonarola, a monk of the house of Medici who grew a cult and was eventually hung and burned simultaneously from the Piazza della Signoria in 1498, had, Claridge said, recommended ice baths for haemorrhages. Through the sixteenth, seventeenth and eighteenth centuries, he wrote, the use of ice water was recommended by the great physicians of the day, including Peter Bernardo, a Capuchin monk who in 1724 travelled to Malta and there cured patients with ice water baths and fasting. Vincenz Priessnitz, Claridge said, was the greatest of that line.

Two years before Priessnitz died, in the winter of 1849, a Bavarian weaver, Sebastian Kneipp, had begun to swim in the waters of the Danube. He did so in what he later described as a state of withered body and withered mind, having nearly died from tuberculosis. By chance he'd picked up a pamphlet on cold-water cures, he recalled, through which he learned of Priessnitz. Kneipp's winter swims electrified him. He began offering treatments from the monastery at Wörishofen, to where villagers travelled as stories of his healing spread. Patients as illustrious as Archduke Franz

Ferdinand and Pope Leo XIII are said to have consulted Kneipp. Alongside cold-water swimming, Kneipp advised his patients to walk barefoot in newly fallen snow. This, he said, was among the simplest ways to harden the body and mind. By the time of his death in 1891, Kneipp's methods had become widespread in Germany, and cold-water bathing was spreading across America.

I remembered the last time I went into cold water, at Brighton beach in November. We'd set out from East Croydon Station as it got light the first Saturday after the clocks went back. By the time we reached Brighton, late the following morning, we'd run sixty miles. Music played from the pier, and lights flashed from the fairground. We congregated on the pebbles where the beach dipped to the sea. My skin turned grey as the water washed over my feet, and I struggled to keep balance. Falling to where the waves broke, the cold was shocking. I let out wooshing sounds, shaking my legs and paddling my arms for warmth. The cold obliterated the stings from the cuts on my ankles, the aches in my legs. When I got out, the sensation of freezing – on the cusp of pain – lingered longest in my feet, which for a few moments stayed tinged blue.

'One is lost', the mountain writer Nan Shepherd said of jumping into the Cairngorm pools, 'then life pours back.' She wrote that the icy water in those mountains had the power to disintegrate the self. Walking, the struggle is slower. The impact builds through hours, days, months, but it too releases a pouring back of life.

Lying on the bathroom floor in Dapaong, with the water flowing over my head, I'm searching again for that feeling: for the cold to obliterate the fever, leave me blank to build back up.

*

I look thin, the waiter says as he waves me off from beside the wooden elephant. I raise to the air the sandwich he thrust into my hand. Children play with tyres on the road. Where the buildings fall away, mist hangs among the thorns. Beyond, there's the outline of the hills.

Many of the trucks have not made the first climb. The shells of vehicles lie along the escarpment road; the seats and tyres stripped, the frames left to rust. Where the slope flattens, boys pass buckets from a stream to the vehicles that managed the ascent. Some have clambered onto the roofs to douse the trucks with cooling water.

I camp at Mango with the truckers, who've gathered beside the gas station for security. I normally start to look for a place to set my tent a couple of hours before dusk. Generally, this means finding a village or a place out of sight from the road. If I'm alone, I look for a spot that's hidden, among trees or behind a lip of rock. The ideal place will be flat ground, with few stones or thorns. I take time to select somewhere I'll feel secure and that will be a pleasant place to sit for the last hour of light. Now, it's a comfort to be around people. At dusk the truckers lay out their mats to pray. We eat around the low flames of makeshift fires.

The embers of the fires still glow at dawn. A low belt of pink light breaks on the horizon. The earth darkens as I move south. There are more bugs and the land greens. To the east, there are mountains. I follow the road onto a ridge, down into the Keran National Park. At the point the hills meet the clouds, the sky is luminous. The forest is dense. Birds of all colours fly among the trees. Butterflies swarm around me. Vast lilies float on pools of dark water. The sky is bright white.

I reach the river late in the afternoon. The village of Nouboulou is on the far bank, the only settlement for twenty miles on my map. I take a track towards the huts. A dead goat lies in a clearing. Chickens pick at the earth around it. The bar is boarded up and the mosque has fallen down. I call out, but no one answers. Something about the place makes me uneasy. I walk to the river and fill my bottles, using my scarf to filter the dirt. I add a drop of salts to each and walk on.

I'm still on the road as dark falls. Because the road is narrow, and I'm not sure if the car will see me, I move from the road whenever a vehicle approaches. There's a drop to the forest. When the lights are on me, I jump. I land in the undergrowth, sometimes falling, sometimes staying upright. I repeat this over and over, covering my arms and legs in cuts.

'Is it possible to say that pain is good?' asked the Dagara writer Malidoma Somé in his book on ritual.

> The Dagara elders would say yes. They believe that a person who has suffered is a person who has heard pain (*won Tuo*). The person hears the pain as a creative action, connecting that person with his or her highest self, which prescribes an alternative to spiritual death. So pain at least teaches us something. It is commotion, e-motion and a call for a rebirth.

## 5

The maize rises high from the base of the hills outside Niamtougou. Streams run through the mud, where men and children work with handheld hoes. In the villages, there are huts of dried earth with grass roofs. The air is warm and wet.

Olaudah Equiano wrote of the land of his childhood looking something like this. His home country was uncommonly green, he said, and around his village, Essaka, every vegetable grew: leafy plantains, yams, beans, wild pineapples, many kinds of pepper. Each family had their own plot. They built their houses with dried earth, dung and roofs of thatched reeds. Inside, the villagers laid muslin covers on their beds, and carved benches from perfumed wood. The whole community came together to build each new home, Equiano recalled, and to fight at the first sign of a threat to the settlement.

I googled the names of the places Equiano described, but was never able to find them. As a child, when he left his homeland for the last time, Equiano said that he'd not heard of the sea, and wasn't aware of the existence of white people, suggesting his home was far from the coast, and from the main trade routes of the day. I later read that even after repeated efforts, no literary historian had been able to trace the location of Equiano's village. All we know from Equiano's narrative is that his home was probably at around the latitude I'm at now, somewhere on the fringes of the old kingdom of Benin, in present-day Nigeria.

Equiano was eleven when he was taken from his village. His captors bound him and his sister with ropes, he wrote, gagging their mouths. After days walking across a forest, his captors sold him to a blacksmith, where he was separated from his sister and set to work. He was repeatedly sold. At Tinmah – in a country he described as more beautiful than any he'd seen – he was bathed in perfume and adopted by the family who purchased him. His mistress was wealthy, he said, and he settled to life in her home, where he ate with the family and played bow and arrow with her son. Without knowing why, he was sold again. He passed plains where cotton grew wild and forests of red wood. He was traded through markets by peoples who filed their teeth sharp like fangs and cut scars into their faces. He was set to work in villages on the banks of a river whose residents lived in canoes.

Seven months after he was first kidnapped, Equiano fainted as he was led onto the deck of the ship. When he came to, he was faced with men of many African nationalities chained together. Someone gave him liquor. When he refused to eat, a ship hand flogged him. Though it was the first time he'd seen the water, and the waves frightened him, he recalled an urge to jump overboard. Nets had been erected to prevent the slaves jumping to their deaths, and Equiano – then eleven or twelve years old – saw many whipped for trying. One man was beaten so severely he died on the spot. Below deck, where Equiano slept, children fell into pools of human waste, sometimes suffocating. Many died of disease. The dying groaned, Equiano wrote, while mothers wailed.

Equiano recalled flying fish jumping across the deck as the ship neared the Caribbean. The clouds, which came and faded on the horizon, appeared like new lands to him. He thought he might be in a parallel world. He remembered believing the white men who manned the ship and flogged the slaves were spirits. How could they make the ship go? he wondered. Why were there no women of their kind? Later, sailing among monk dolphins, which came so close they blew water onto the deck, he imagined the dolphins as rulers of the sea, that they controlled the winds which he'd learned guided the boat through the waves.

Equiano's is one of few first-hand accounts that survive by someone shipped as a slave in the trans-Atlantic trade. I don't know what I expected when I picked up Equiano's book. I thought I'd find it hard going, that the accounts of his treatment would be difficult to face. But in parts of the book I forgot it was an account of slavery at all. As Equiano arrived in Falmouth in 1757, having been acquired by a British navy officer in Virginia, and saw snow for the first time; as he sailed to the Orkneys, and then to Greenland, where the boat came up against great ice cliffs, and whales circled, and the sun never set, Equiano's account read more like an adventure story. Perhaps it was because, writing for a contemporary British audience, Equiano wanted to avoid too much about English cruelty, or maybe it's that he refused to be defined by it. At times though, as he returned to the West Indies in the 1760s – to the Bahamas, St Kitts, Montserrat – where he saw slave owners rape ten-year-old girls, and slice off men's ears for perceived insubordination; and in Savannah, Georgia, where a drunk doctor beat him to within an inch of his life, the reader plunges with him into the world of a slave.

Equiano bought his freedom in 1766. When he'd finished his autobiography, many of London's most celebrated figures subscribed, including John Wesley, who shortly before he died, passed the book to William Wilberforce. Equiano's narrative was reprinted multiple times, and became a literary sensation. Through his activism he helped end British involvement in the slave trade, and in such a way his life and narrative became part of that wider struggle.

Reading of Edith Bone in her cell, Richard Byrd on the ice, Thoreau in his cabin, I came to see struggle as something that could make a person. It was part of what I hoped for walking. But faced with the journeys of Olaudah Equiano – of a people and an era who suffered the most extreme hardship – the idea of struggling as a way to build up a person collapses. For the men and women on those ships, however hard they struggled, most met only ruin or death.

6

At Bar le Citoyen, on the banks of the mud river in Kara, the waiter brings a beer. I've walked 150 miles since Dapaong, and it's the first cold drink I've had in weeks. The bottle is ice cold, with beads of condensation running down the neck. The waiter says *long journey*, and laughs, popping open the drink. I set down my pack. The air is breezy, the table shaded, so although it's the hottest time of day, I feel cool. The muscles in my legs ache a good ache, a sensation that's not pain, only a knowing of the miles behind.

I've been walking so long each day, I haven't written. I write what comes to mind of the past days: the fear walking into the dark from Nouboulou; the cloth trader driving south from Ouagadougou who told me I'd die on that road in the night, and dropped me at the bus station in Kandé, ten miles on; the hillside tracks through Niamtougou, Farende, Pya; the strange auditoriums that rose from the mud villages in those hills, built to celebrate the home region of Eyadéma, who'd claimed to walk, Messiah-like, from the flames of the crashed plane.

The waiter brings a plate of guinea fowl. I take a last swig of beer. The man opposite dips his hands in a bowl of water. He shakes them dry, before resuming his meal. I eat like a bushman, he says, meeting my eye. It's better to eat with one's hands: to feel the meat and the bones.

When the man has finished his food, and we've sat across from each other, he gives me his card, which says *Professor en Archéologie, Université d'Abomey-Calavi*.

He asks if I know the story of the Taung Child.

It's one of the first archaeological stories teachers teach, he says. Like Newton and the apple. The child's skull was unearthed by miners at a lime works in South Africa in the early twentieth century. It ended up on the desk of a member of the quarry management, who used it as a paperweight. Following a chance sighting of another fossil, on the mantlepiece of a quarry director, the skull was sent, along with the other fossils gathered from the site, to an anthropologist, Raymond Dart.

Now we know much about the skull, the archaeologist says. Decades of analysis show that it sat beneath the face of a girl of three or four years old; that she lived two million years ago; and – puncture marks around her eye-sockets suggest – that she was killed by an eagle. What caught the attention of Raymond Dart, though, was the skull's bone structure: the small teeth, the flattish face, the position of the hole at the skull's base, through which the spinal cord passed to the brain. These characteristics, Dart believed, indicated the Taung Child to be a member of a to-that-point unknown species, a link between human's older ape ancestors and modern man.

But when, in February 1925, Dart proposed to the academic community a fossil that was such a link species, his theory was denounced. The pre-eminent paleontologists of the day – men such as Sir Arthur Smith Woodward, Curator of Geology at London's Natural History Museum, and Sir Arthur Keith, Conservator of the Hunterian Museum of the Royal College of Surgeons – rejected Dart's hypothesis, saying that, far from a revolutionary species, the skull belonged to an infant gorilla, and offered nothing more significant than this to evolutionary history.

Woodward and Keith had themselves been involved in a momentous and controversial find the decade preceding the Taung Child discovery. After Charles Dawson, an amateur archaeologist dug up fragments of a skull resembling a human in a bed of Pleistocene gravel near the village of Piltdown in Sussex, Dawson took his find to Woodward. Woodward reconstructed the skull and, in December 1912, presented it with Dawson to the Geological Society in London. The pair argued that the bones belonged to a human-like being that had lived 500,000 years before: that it was the missing link species between ape and man.

The Taung Child and Piltdown Man told different stories of human evolution. Piltdown Man had a large cranium, but teeth that were more ape-like than human. The form of Piltdown Man's skull suggested that the break characteristic which first defined human from monkey was its large brain, and the emerging intellect that suggested. The skull indicated too that the evolutionary leap from ape to human had taken place in Europe, and that, by extension, the first man could be called an Englishman.

The Taung Child contradicted this. She had a small brain, and the position of the hole at the base of her skull – which allowed the spinal cord to feed into the brain in such a way as to keep her head balanced while she walked on two feet – suggested that she had walked before she thought like a human. If the Taung Child was indeed the link species Dart claimed, the thing that first defined human from ape, was not thinking, but walking on two feet, and the first human had evolved not in Europe, but in Africa.

The two skulls, and the conflicting theories that accompanied them, remained the subject of debate for thirty years. It wasn't until nearly four decades after the Piltdown find, and twenty-five years after Dart published his first paper on the Taung Child, that a team from Oxford uncovered Piltdown Man as a fraud. Someone had taken the jaw of an orangutan, teeth from a chimpanzee and a human skull, and scattered them among other fossils in the gravel beds at Piltdown. Before depositing the bones, the person playing the hoax had filed down the chimpanzee's teeth so they looked more human and, to give the fossils an appearance of antiquity, stained the skull with potassium. The hoaxer had, it later transpired, even left caveman tools among the fossils, one resembling a prehistoric cricket bat.

As the archaeologist finishes his story, it occurs to me that perhaps he is saying the same thing as the man in Tamale, who drank at the Jungle Café and told me, on learning of my walk, that he hoped he wouldn't hear me one day on the BBC, telling the world about Africa, as if, like so many foreigners, I thought I knew the continent better than its own people. But when the man pays for his food, and gets up to leave, he says that he told me about the Taung Child because he hoped it might be a comfort for me – walking so far – to know that walking is what made us human at the start.

*To Dassa-Zoumé, a town set among forty-one hills, on the edge of the old kingdom of Dahomey. Every August, one of the largest mass pilgrimages in West Africa ends at Dassa. The road from Kara crosses the border to Benin, then south through the hills of central Benin.*

The road goes east to Ouaké, on the border to Benin. Kara is quiet at this time. There are just the noises of the cocks, women sweeping mats, the water in the stream. The air is grey and mists cover the hills. It's cold. For the first time on the journey, I walk in my jacket. I pull my scarf around my face.

The road passes dense forest and hills of red mud. The mist has thickened to fog and rain falls. A woman selling petrol arranges her bottles. Others lay out tomatoes, dried fish, sacks of charcoal. Children walk to school in oversize backpacks, singing songs. Scooters pass in clouds of black smoke.

Slowly, the mist burns away. The sweat on my shirt chills in the air when I take off my jacket. I stop for food at a bar called Dieu Donne Fufu, at another called New Harlem. The walls of the bars are painted with the red of Coca-Cola, the green of the *Rassemblement du Peuple Togolais*, snakes and whales of many colours. The hours pass quickly. The road to Benin rolls east.

'Cotonou is a pretty little town,' Ryszard Kapuściński wrote of Benin's main city, 'but a boring one'. 'Its sole real attraction', he said, 'is the revolution, which occurs only once every few months'.

By the end of 1965, the year Kapuściński recalled that conversation, Benin was in the midst of its third revolution in two years. The newly independent country would see seven more over the next seven years. During this time – the country's first decade after independence from France – Benin was known by its old name, *Dahomey*, after the Fon kingdom which sat within its borders.

It was Mathieu Kérékou, the soldier who took power in the coup of October 1972, who renamed the country Benin. Kérékou, a Marxist who would rule the country for thirty years, adopted the nickname *the Chameleon*, a symbol of life in Benin. 'The branch will not break in the arms of the chameleon,' Kérékou said on taking power. He had the animal carved into his cane.

Kérékou named his country after the kingdom of Benin, which was 300 miles to the east, in the rainforests beyond the Niger Delta. That kingdom emerged sometime around the twelfth century. Its early Edo founders, who cleared a patch of forest on which to establish the city's first huts, came to be known as *Ogiso*, the kings from the sky. By the sixteenth century, the kingdom they'd built controlled trade across a vast stretch of coast, reaching from the mouth of the Niger River 500 miles west to the Volta Delta. European travellers from the period report a state capital with a moat and high walls; oil lanterns burning in the night streets; a palace court as large as the Dutch city of Haarlem, then a great trading centre.

As the old kingdom of Benin fell into decline, the kingdom of Dahomey, which would become known the world over and whose name Kérékou would discard, was rising up. Dahomey traces its roots to the village of Tado, where, some time in the distant past, a panther is said to have turned into a man. The man became a great hunter and met a beautiful girl, on her way to bathe at a spring. They had a child and the child became a king. The king had three sons who, on their father's deathbed, quarrelled over who would inherit the kingdom. Each son left his father's domain to find his own. The first built his palace at Allada; the second at Porto Novo; the third, named

Dogbagri, came to the Abomey plateau, to the lands that would become Dahomey.

It was Dogbagri's son, Dakodonu, who founded the city of Abomey, the Dahomean capital. When Dakodonu requested land from Dan, a local chief, Dan is said to have laughed at Dakodonu, asking if he should open up his belly so Dakodonu could build his city there. National legend says Dakodonu killed Dan on the spot, building his palace in the place he died, and burying his remains beneath the foundations. The kingdom that grew from that first palace was Dahomey, which in Fon means *inside the belly of Dan*.

During the seventeenth and eighteenth centuries, Dahomey's palaces multiplied. Each Dahomean king undertook to leave the kingdom larger than the one he inherited. Dahomey took control of the coast's main slaving ports, including Ouidah, and became a dominant power in West Africa's slave trade. Some estimates suggest that as many as every fifth slave exported in the Atlantic trade passed through Dahomey's supply chains.

During the time of the Annual Customs, the whole city gathered at Abomey's palace to pay homage to the king; to watch the soldiers parade; and to witness human sacrifices. It's said the deceased were sent to the afterworld with questions for the first kings, whose wills were read by priests in trance. As late as 1864, when Richard Burton passed through Abomey, thirty-nine people, according to Burton's account, were publicly executed during the Annual Customs. Through its role in the slave trade, perhaps somewhat embellished stories of the Annual Customs, and accounts of the *Mino* – the band of the king's wives, trained initially as elephant hunters, but who later became bodyguards to the king – Dahomey grew infamous in Europe. 'Beware, beware the Bight of Benin,' children sang in eighteenth-century England, 'for few come out where many go in ...'

By the time Béhanzin, the last king of independent Dahomey, came to power in 1889, the kingdom was fragile. With the abolition of the slave trade, Dahomey had lost its main source of income. And over the final decades of the nineteenth century, as the French settled in the key coastal towns, it faced losing sovereignty. Béhanzin led the last stand. He tore up the treaty which, twenty years earlier, had given the French control of Cotonou port, and sent the army to block French advances inland. He led two wars against French colonial forces, but eventually lost Abomey, setting fire to the city's palaces before retreating north. He was later captured leading a guerrilla resistance, and exiled to Martinique. Béhanzin died in exile in Algeria in 1906.

Perhaps through the mingling of so many peoples in Dahomey, and the coming together of so many spiritual traditions – Fon, Yoruba, Edo, Ewe, Ashanti and others – the religion of the Dahomean people, Vodou, came to be among the most followed traditional African religion, with adherents all over the world. It was a religion which, soon after he came to power in 1972, Mathieu Kérékou sought to drive out of Benin. Eager to place in positions of influence people loyal to him across the country, Kérékou purged the Vodou priests and healers who practised in the villages. He did so under the banner of Marxism, rallying the people to root out those he called witches and sorcerers who, he said, held the country back.

Although Vodou was pushed underground under Kérékou, and the French before him, the practices endured. Since Kérékou fell from power, after the country came again to the brink of revolution, people have spoken of a Vodou renaissance. Millions still follow the religion in Benin. At Ouidah, each new year, thousands gather to celebrate the national Vodou festival. And in the old kingdom towns on the road south to there – Savalou, Dassa Zoumé, Abomey – Vodou remains strong.

At the border, the officials give me a seat in the shade and ask me questions. What is your nationality? Where have you travelled from? Where are you going? Why do you want to enter Benin?

The questions become stranger.

Where did you learn to speak French? Is your stick a javelin? Are you a soldier? Who pays you? Do you carry medicine? Are you on Facebook? Will you pass Kétou? Where do you sleep? What happens when it rains? How is it that you are white but too poor to buy a bicycle? How do you guard against wild animals?

I leave with a sheet of phone numbers.

Any problems, call. And do not take the dirt road to Pénéssoulou, the guard says. It's not safe.

So I take the sealed road east to Djougou. It's further, but at this stage an extra day is meaningless. I no longer feel my pack. The sun no longer troubles me. I know to rest for twenty minutes late in the morning and again in the middle of the afternoon. I am patient with the children who run behind in each village. I always carry coins as no one has change. When people ask where I am going, I say the next town. Otherwise they will say it's impossible and ask a thousand questions.

When a passing scooter stops to offer a lift, I know to say that I am doing sports. This is the only thing I can say that will leave the driver satisfied that I don't need help.

I know that whenever I ask for directions the answer will be *là-bas*. I bow when I meet someone older than me. I'm used to eating with my hands. I know that I cannot rise from my haunches until the old man gives the signal. I know that the men with guns will not harm me. I know that cigarettes cost 20p a pack, a bottle of beer 50p, a fish head 15p. I know to eat the fish head whole.

When the flies come, and they come in droves, I bind my scarf into a rope and whip it over my shoulders, like a tail, until the flies disperse. Because of the scarf people think I am an Arab. When I say I am British, people look back blankly. The outside world is Nigeria, Côte d'Ivoire and, further off, China. But above all the outside world is France. People believe Paris is paradise and ask me to take them there.

I understand now that time has little value. Here, money has value, but company has the greatest value of all. More than anything, it is others that people search for and cherish. I'm rarely alone because people want to talk.

If I sit to eat someone will sit beside me. If I walk among strangers, they take hold of my hands. Whenever there is music there is dancing. Children dance from dawn till dusk. *To dance is to spin the sun,* the Ewe say. The dead return to dance once a year. They come in the robes of a Yoruba divinity and chase the living with sticks. They are called back from the forest by a man in white cloth softly beating a drum.

In some West African languages there's no distinction between the living and the dead. In Gur dialects, spoken in northern Ghana, *I am going to give father a drink* and *I am going to water his grave* are the same. Whenever a drink is poured, the first drop is splashed to the earth for the ancestors: *A la terre Afrique*, the men say.

If I take out my iPod a crowd forms because it's beautiful. When the sailors smashed the rocks at Elmina, fighting broke out. The world came into being by the union of a serpent and a rainbow. In the desert, life started as a drop of milk; in the forest as a child of red earth. The lives of the unborn rest in the leaves of silk cottons. Wisdom lives in a calabash buried beneath a tree. Some spirits receive only blood. Some priests speak the language of the birds. Some stones have souls. The sticks the herders carry are harder than iron. The herders will walk for days, for weeks, for months, for years. If there's nuclear war, or pandemic, and life comes close to ending, it will be the nomads, deep in their deserts, who survive and build back up the world again.

In Ga, rain and God are the same word. When the rain comes, the keepers of the houses go out with pots to catch the water. When the trucks overheat on the hill roads, children come with buckets and douse them back to life. If a woman has twins and one dies, she will bind a wooden doll to her midriff and carry it everywhere she goes from the day of the burial. Twins are sacred. Often people ask if it is forbidden in my country to have more than one child. They say this is how it is in China. *A bad place.* If someone has twins in China, do they cut off one of the heads?

At the crossroads there are policemen instead of traffic lights. They wear blue jackets, white gloves, and stand like statues in the chaos. On the walls of the old buildings there are murals of birds pecking their backs. The bird is there to remind passers-by not to forget what came before. On the edges of the villages there are horned mounds to ward off evil. At the junctions there are billboards of men walking through lightning.

Sometimes I'm asked if I'm a spy, sometimes Peace Corps, sometimes an explorer. Some people can read a revolution on a man's face before it happens. Some dance or drum or walk to a place where their mind rises to a different place. The Sufis call this *fana*, passing away. The law of the road is based on size. 4x4s barge cars off the tracks; cars send scooters to the mud; women with basins on their heads give way to everything. To be on foot is to live in the dirt.

When I feel my hands burning, I bind them. If my feet start to bleed, I douse them in iodine. When the dust gets thick, I pull my scarf across my mouth. When the rain comes, I sit with the old men beneath the trees and wait.

## 8

In the time of Mahommah Baquaqua, the city of Djougou stood on a plain of high grasses, on which lion and elephant roamed. When the grasses had grown to a certain height, the hunters of the city, and those from villages across the plains, gathered with bows and flames. They formed a circle, Baquaqua wrote – miles wide – and set light to the grasses. As the flames spread, the hunters moved forward, using wet leaves to protect their feet from the scorched ground. The animals fled the smoke towards the circle's centre, until there was nowhere left to flee, and the hunters killed everything.

The city to which they returned with their meat was surrounded by a hedge of thorns, so thick, Baquaqua wrote, as to be impassable. Beyond the thorns was a moat, filled during the rains, and behind it, a wall of red clay, to which six gates gave access. The doors were named after their keepers, Baquaqua said, who were known through the town as Fathers of the Gates.

Baquaqua's account of life in Djougou at the start of the nineteenth century, written in collaboration with the abolitionist Samuel Moore, was full of what seem now to be curious details of the old city, a place of which there's little trace on the road I'm walking: past the yard where the buses stop, to the Algerian motel on the edge of town. In Baquaqua's time, a wide avenue ran to the king's palace. The townspeople lived in mud bungalows, red like the city walls, with no windows. In the markets, Baquaqua recalled, blacksmiths worked bellows created from a goat skin cut whole from the animal, combined with a gun barrel, through which air flowed when the goat's legs were moved. Women pounded yam flour in vast mortars, cut from a hollowed tree, which was rolled by hand from the forest by a great group of men under the king's instruction. Salt was transported from Sab-ba, two months' journey away, to be exchanged for cattle, ivory or slaves.

Baquaqua – at the time a member of the king's court – was sold into slavery in the 1840s. He'd been plied with grain wine, he remembered, on a visit to a neighbouring village, and woke bound. His captives tied a six-foot stake to his back and walked him to the sea. They shipped him to Brazil, where a baker from Pernambuco acquired him. He tried to escape but was caught and beaten. He attempted suicide, but was pulled from the river into which he'd jumped. Under a new master, he was taken on a trade ship to New York – then a free place – where he managed to escape. Baquaqua's biography is the only first hand account known to survive the millions of people taken as slaves from Africa to Brazil.

Beyond the walled motel, south out of Djougou, paths of red dust reach from the road. I try to imagine the early journeys that ground these tracks into the earth. The men who walked the salt from Sab-ba; the workers who rolled the trunks from the forest for the mortars; the hunters who took bows and flaming branches into the savannah; the townspeople who walked each day to the stream in which, Baquaqua wrote, water flowed that was white as milk; and the slaves who, like Baquaqua, had stakes strapped to their backs, and would never walk the tracks from their homes again.

The ground is all memoranda and signatures, Ralph Emerson said: history written into the earth by those who walked before. What would Emerson have made of the dust tracks off the road south from Djougou? Most places I've walked in my life, paths are associated with freedom. I like to think of the peoples who first broke the ground: what made them go that way, whether they could have imagined that over generations the steps they took would be reprinted again and again, until the way on which they'd first struck out had been carved for centuries, sometimes thousands of years, into rock and dust.

I visualise the path across Port Meadow near my home. I've run and walked it so many times I can recall it in detail. To reach the path I cross the canal. I pass men walking their dogs, others wheeling barrows to the allotments. The old path starts at the gate beyond the railway track, where the meadow begins.

The meadow is often flooded in winter, sometimes frozen over. If I run late in the day, as the sun sinks behind the woods on the escarpment, the water looks black, and it's hard to discern the grazing animals from the grey light. The horses appear from nowhere. I take an old track of grey stone, parallel to a ditch. The track is raised from the mud and, even when the water is at its highest, is passable. After a third of a mile, the track joins a narrower path, which descends to a wooden bridge across the river.

Poplars and oak grow on the bank. Beside where trees have fallen, rabbits emerge from the brambles. The water is clear, the riverbed sandy. In summer there are flies. The path goes by a boat yard, then a pub, a lock, the ruins of an abbey. From the village of Wolvercote, on the meadow's northern side, the path returns across the soaked ground, to re-join the stone track.

As a child, I filled that track with stories. I visualised on it soldiers from the jerky footage we saw in history lessons, marching from the trenches, muddied, bandaged, smoking cigarettes. I saw families on wooden carts making their way west into the dust; shepherds with cattle descending from the hills. I became part of their journeys as I dawdled behind my family on the meadow. I wondered who'd put the grey stones into the mud and why. Sometimes the track appeared when I was far from it. As I watched *The Woman in Black*, the hooves on the causeway playing out through the hushed theatre, the audience quiet with fear, I saw the track across the meadow.

Before those stones were set, the path was carved by herders, who've led cattle across the meadow for thousands of years. Local legend says that the ancient peoples of Oxford were given the ground in return for defending the country from Danish raiders in the tenth century. Seven hundred years later, people raced horses on the tracks. In the 1980s, people congregated on the meadow for raves. Now, most walk there for walking's sake; they go, like me, to feel freer. Each day, new footsteps keep the stones bare. In the way Emerson thought about it, each is adding their signature to the land.

At a visitor centre on the shore of the Langebaan Lagoon, South Africa, replicas of the earliest preserved human footprints ever found, believed to belong to a woman who walked to the crest of a sand dune on that shore 117,000 years ago, are presented in a slab of grey concrete. The palaeontologists who discovered the foot-prints of the woman, now known as Eve, estimated that she stood a little over five feet tall, and was walking in a storm. Soon after she passed a steep section of dune, dry sand blew into the wet prints she'd left. Over the follow-ing millennia, sand and shells built up over the dunes, burying the footprints beneath rock. No one knows where the woman was walking; whether it was the start of a great journey or steps on a plainer daily ritual.

There is a clearer story for the mudflat footprints at Happisburgh, Norfolk. The fifty footprints, which belonged to a mix of hominid adults and children, were revealed after storm tides washed away sediment in 2013. The walkers had left the marks 850,000 years earlier, a time when East Anglia's marshes and clay ridges were rich in food to forage, but dangerous, as wolves, hyena and sabre-toothed cats roamed the pine forests beyond the estuary's banks. The group was walking south down the estuary, perhaps in search of lugworms and crab.

I like the idea of coming after those who walked before, wearing the path down, in some way forming a connec-tion. Here, though, on the road south out of Djougou, the most prominent long-distance journeys are those of men and women like Baquaqua, who were walked as slaves. Because of the people who came before me, the dominant history of the paths here are not about freedom, but pain: the paths are threads to a violent past.

9

At the edge of Bassila, a sprawl of corrugated roofs, rust and smoke, an old man holds a chain across the road. The tar is caked in mud. The man wears no shoes, and has a rifle at his side, a bullet belt across his chest. He slackens the chain to let me pass. At the roundabout beyond, hawkers sell electric toys, Chinese medicines, plantains on fronds. Children dance among the vendors, cartwheeling through the dust before the mosque. Meagre piles of coal and tomatoes are laid on wooden stools, beside mounds of melon and yam. I buy a portion of charred goat from a man with a barrel stove. He wraps the meat in paper torn from a cement bag. I eat as I walk.

It's spitting with warm rain on the road from Bassila. The rocks that rise from the trees glisten in the wet. Straw roof huts steam in the humid air. Women sit in lines on the roadside, breaking rocks to gravel. Boys run from the verge shouting 'Cadeau, cadeau!' I sweat heavily. In my right hand I hold my stick; in my left, my scarf, which I whip across my shoulders to clear the flies. To Dassa-Zoumé, it's 100 miles. Every seven or eight hours, there's a village. I walk from Bassila to Prékété; from Prékété to Pira; from Pira to Banté; from Banté to Agoua. The days lose definition. I see the sun rise, peak and fall from the road.

There's a point in most long journeys when everything beyond burns away. You're left with just the ground ahead, whatever will to keep going survives. There's something primal about this state. You become wolf-like, mindless for the ground, no longer stopping to eat, to fix the sores on your feet, to wipe the blood from the cuts. The drawing down of stamina obliterates all feeling. You chase the road for its own sake.

I remember the long climb up Kapruner Törl. The race had started at 10 p.m. on a Friday night. I gathered with the other runners in the town square, perhaps 400 of us. The organisers played music as we waited, while the townspeople, returning from dinner, gathered to see us off. We huddled by the barriers as the announcer led a countdown, our breath visible in the mountain air.

A steep track led through the forest to the mountain. It was unusually humid, and thick-bodied flies were drawn from the pines to our headlamps. We each settled into the motion of the climb, using poles to give rhythm to our steps. Sweat poured from me, which – once out of the forest – was freezing on the skin beneath my wet shirt. I stopped to refill my bottles at the aid station and take a cup of salty soup, then headed on into the night.

My stomach collapsed. I stopped to throw up, past caring if other competitors could see me from the trail. I reached the final ascent of the first high pass, which was coated in hardened snow, shortly before dawn. The sky was grey then. The steepness of the slope and the difficulty of the ground meant I had to break every fifteen minutes to catch my breath. A marshal was camped at the summit. He said something in German. The sun was rising and the glacier beneath us went silver. The trail passed grey boulders and lakes of black water. As the rim of the sun rose over the peak, I took a photo of the long chain of head torches passing through the rocks.

Runner after runner passed me on the descent. The trail was narrow and I stood aside to let each by. For the next five hours I moved painfully slowly. My knees couldn't handle the strain of the downs. At the aid stations I couldn't eat. I tried to vomit, but nothing came. I began to worry I'd miss the cut off time and be disqualified. By late morning the following day, as the track climbed through the scree, I was moving at little more than two kilometres an hour, less than half normal walking speed. I hadn't slept for thirty hours.

A helicopter landed as I reached the base of the second climb. Someone had fallen into the gorge, a marshal said. I forced down a piece of bread and took some codeine. The trail passed grass meadows, along a shaded track through the trees. As the painkillers kicked in, I began to run again. I counted each runner I passed, feeling a euphoria I knew couldn't last.

The race mid-point, at sixty kilometres, was at the gymnasium in the town of Kals, in a wide valley beneath the mountain. Inside, it looked as if there'd been a natural disaster. Runners, many in silver blankets, were sprawled across the floors. Marshals served plates of hot food and doctors attended those in need. I ate a bowl of spaghetti and ran back into the sunlight. From there, the trail followed a river, to the base of Grossglockner, the last climb. I felt close to delirious. *Be like the wolf*, I said to myself over and over, as I tried to force myself back into a run. Perhaps two hours later, I reached a hut below where the mountain began to climb steeply. A man in lederhosen came out with a keg of beer. Runners lay in the grass around him. The race is over, he said, handing me a glass. There's a storm on the mountain. I stumbled through the gate, watching a participant descend the track from the mountain. We'd come ninety kilometres and none of us had crossed the finish line. We walked an hour back along the path to the road. Waiting in the rain for a coach back to Kaprun, I wondered what we'd been looking for on the mountain. What had we taken from it?

10

The night rain has cut patterns in the mud on the road into Savalou. I stop at the Hotel Le Musso, which has walls of pink stucco and a pool of caiman in the yard. An old man, in a cowboy hat with the word JERUSALEM written in gold above the brim, sits alone in the hotel bar. Lights spin from a disco ball above him.

Tomorrow kings from across West Africa come to Savalou, the man says. Obas from Nigeria; Duala chiefs from Cameroon; princes from Gabon and Brazzaville; the heads of the royal families of Allada, Porto Novo, Ouidah. The Asantehene has travelled from Kumasi in sandals of solid gold.

Colonel Gaddafi once came with them to Savalou. He drove in a convoy of a hundred Land Cruisers, the man says: soldiers on the vehicle roofs, flags flying above the headlights. The roads were cleared for a thousand miles, so the convoy never stopped as it drove across the desert. The journey must have taken days, he says, but that wasn't the point. In every village from Tripoli to Savalou, the people saw the Great King pass.

Gaddafi began to call himself that, the man says – *the Great King* – in what would be the latter years of his rule. He wanted to build a United Africa, modelled on the USA, with a single currency and army. Power would be given to the traditional leaders, who Gaddafi saw as rightful heirs to the kingdoms of pre-colonial Africa.

The king of Savalou was one of those heirs, the man says, a supporter of Gaddafi's vision. He was close to Gaddafi. In return for the king's support, Gaddafi did much for Savalou. He laid the sealed roads, sponsored the town's clinics, made refurbishments to the palace. Even now Gaddafi is dead, the kings he gathered still convene. This year they come to Savalou, to celebrate the harvest of the first yam.

The man in the hotel bar, who I come to know as Monsieur Antoine, puts me in the care of Armand, the Royal Photographer. Armand will see to it that I have everything I need during my stay, Monsieur Antoine says. I am to see the cutting of the yam; to participate in the dances and the sacrifices; to meet the king.

The day before the festival, Armand takes me to a temple out of town: a small building of grey breeze blocks in a clearing. The temple was built to commemorate the village's founding ancestor, says the priest, who wears a shirt printed with snakes and crosses. It was consecrated to Sakpata, god of the earth.

It takes a moment to adjust to the light. All along the wall there are statues. Candles and shampoo bottles stand beside them. A snake is painted in faded ink along the upper wall. The python lay between the land and the sea, the priest says, before there were gods or people. As the snake stirred, it pushed up the space above the earth to form the sky. Its movement created sparks which became the stars. The python coiled across the earth, forging mountains, rivers and valleys. It let out waters which filled rivers and spread life. With the first rains, a rainbow rose. The rainbow joined the snake and the pair became one.

In Haiti, to where Vodou travelled with slaves, people call the rainbow Ayida-Weddo, the spirit of water, fertility and fire. Her snake companion is Damballah, whose origins come from the python god at Ouidah. In Haitian temples, Damballah is sometimes drawn with the head of Moses and a body of seven coils. Like many of the Vodou gods of Haiti, Damballah became associated with a saint. On the plantations, those taken as slaves from West Africa were prohibited from practising the religion of their homelands, so they used Catholic icons, given to them by French priests, to represent their gods. To this day, icons of St Patrick are found in shrines to Damballah in Haiti, showing a picture of the saint driving the snakes out of Ireland. The rainbow spirit, Ayida-Weddo, is often beside him, represented by the Virgin Mary.

At the height of the slave trade, in the late-eighteenth century, the French-controlled territory that is now Haiti – then Saint-Domingue – was the largest sugar producer in the world. The Europeans, who had first arrived on the island in 1492, and quickly killed off the Taíno Indians who lived there, had cleared plains across the country to plant the crop, for which demand in Europe was soaring. They dug irrigation canals to carry water from the mountains, and built boiling houses to process the cane. By the 1790s, 450,000 slaves were living in Saint-Domingue – many taken from villages in Benin – alongside a population of 55,000 free people. Conditions on the plantations were so inhumane, and disease so rife, that each year between 5 and 10 per cent of Saint-Domingue's slave population are estimated to have died.

Perhaps, under these conditions, it would have seemed inevitable to the slave masters that the people would rise up. But those who ran the plantations seemed unprepared for the events that unfolded in the summer of 1791. The Haitian revolution began, it's said, at a ceremony in the woods in the north of the island, the Bois Caïman, on a night in August. A priest and slave leader called Dutty Boukman, originally from Senegambia, was presiding over the ceremony, when a storm rose from the mountains above the woods. Within a month, tens of thousands of slaves had joined the uprising, and hundreds of plantations had been burned. A bloody conflict followed, in which hundreds of thousands of revolutionaries, slave owners and French soldiers died. The revolution shattered the illusion of the slave masters' supremacy in front of the world. Historians see the Haitian revolution, and the emergence of Haiti as a free state, as the pivotal moment in the collapse of the slave trade.

Some of the leaders of that revolution – notably the resistance general and first ruler of independent Haiti, Jean-Jacques Dessalines – have since passed into the pantheon of Vodou spirits. In Haiti, Dessalines is revered as *Ogou Desalin*, a spirit of strength and resistance linked to the old West African warrior god, Gu, whose axe-head stands, among bottles of gin and perfume, in the temple at Savalou.

Many of the spirits which have shrines in Savalou's temple were carried to Haiti, where some merged with Yoruba and Ashanti divinities, and others with Catholic saints, to form the gods of Haitian Vodou. The spirits which came from Dahomey are known as *Rada* in Haiti, while those that emerged later on the island are known as *Petro*. Arising in the brutal conditions of the slave plantations, the Petro spirits are seen as having fiercer temperaments than the benevolent Rada of Africa.

It was in Haiti that Vodou grew prominent in the Western imagination. Much of this was down to stories which spread in America in the first half of the twentieth century. In films like *White Zombie*, released in 1932, which told the story of an American woman who travelled to Haiti with her fiancée, Vodou became associated in the American imagination with black magic. In that movie, Murder Legendre, a Vodou priest who runs a sugar mill operated by the dead, is hired by a suitor of the American to turn her into a zombie as part of a plan to entrap her.

*White Zombie* triggered a flurry of zombie movies, many of which, like the 1943 release, *I Walked with a Zombie*, featured Americans travelling to Haiti and being terrorised by Vodou priests. In popular culture, Vodou became associated with voodoo dolls, zombies, black magic. As recently as 2010, the American evangelist, Pat Robertson, claimed that the Haitian earthquake, which killed 100,000 people in January of that year, was divine retribution for the gathering at the Bois Caïman, which he described as a pact with the devil.

But Vodou is just a religion, the priest at Savalou says, no different to those of the East or West. It shares a way of looking at the world common to most traditional religions. There is the creator: Nyame to the Ashanti, Olodumare to the Yoruba, Mawu in Vodou. Then the spirits who control the earth's forces: gods of rivers and fertility, sickness and death, iron and trees: Abosom to the Ashanti, Orisha for the Yoruba, Vodhun for followers of Vodou. Next are the ancestors, guardians of each people's history and identity. Last are the smaller spirits, who live in the forests, rocks and streams. Vodou, the priest says, is about harmony between these forces and humankind.

*

Hundreds of townspeople have gathered at the palace for the ceremony of the first yam. The king sits with his wife on a velvet throne beneath a muslin umbrella. A member of the Ministry of Culture has come from Porto Novo; the American ambassador from Cotonou. The dignitaries sit on wooden chairs beside the kings. The townspeople stand in the sun around them. Goats sit on the tops of the palace walls.

Insignia of Savalou's rulers are painted on the walls beneath. A buffalo for Savalou's founding king, Soha Gbaguidi; others of reptiles and elephants; four hands lifting a dove to the sky for Tossoh, the current ruler. The chief of palace security, a huge man in white robes, leads Armand and me through the crowds. We pass a statue of women in chains, another of a rain-god shrine, onto which, the chief of security says, the palace priests drain pig's blood in times of drought.

The last statue we pass is a lion with a bone in its jaws. The king built this after Gaddafi died, Armand says. Tossoh's enemies had taunted him after Gaddafi's death. Without his powerful patron, they said, the king would be no more than an impoverished chief. The message of the statue is that as a lion always eats meat, so the king will always be great.

We take our seats beside the lion. Nine Yoruba dancers enter the courtyard, holding bull tails in white-gloved hands. They bow before the king. The chains on their ankles clink above the drums. On their crowns there are snakes, horses, birds. These symbols remember Gelede, daughter of Yemoja, the mother of the world. It's said the dance was first danced by Yemoja at the beginning of time to make life grow in her belly. The ambassador applauds as the masked figures surround him.

For the preparation of the first yam, we process to an inner courtyard, away from the crowds. The head priest holds a bottle of palm oil; his assistants knives and a bottle of gin. On their haunches, the men cut the yam and douse it in liquor. Chanting, they throw the pieces to the shrines.

II

At dusk Monsieur Antoine takes me to the dancing of the *egungun*. The first dancers to come wear bright cloths and masks of white muslin. Each is accompanied by a minder, a young man with a thin stick, who tries to guide the masked figure. Hundreds of onlookers wait in the close, dusk air. Those across from where we sit, on the far side of the square, have their faces pressed against the wire meshing. Above us, children watch from the branches of the mango trees. The crowds part for Monsieur Antoine as we walk from the track. Some of the young men square up to me. Monsieur Antoine keeps a hand on my shoulder, as if to show, to anyone who might doubt it, that I'm here under his protection. He takes his seat on a bench at the front.

The robes of the dancers now coming to the square are elaborate. Mannequin heads and animal horns have been stitched to their backs and lapels. The costumes mean the dancers, who represent the dead, lose all semblance of human form as they move. They charge the crowd with whips, triggering stampedes which fill the air with dust. The young men taunt them, trying to draw them from the square, laughing as the whips come down around their flaying legs. The old belief is that if any part of the *egungun* cloth touches the skin of a living person, that person will die. The minders closely track the masked figures.

Across the square, a tall man emerges, robed head-to-toe in deer hide, antlers hanging from his back. Behind him, a figure in black follows. He wears a crown of chain and bone, and walks slowly, as if weighed down by metal. The dancers still as he passes. The young men fade into the crowd. Everything becomes hushed. A man in a football shirt leads a calf by a rope. He binds the animal's feet and presses it to the ground beside the pole. The calf has terror in its eyes. A heavy-set man in butcher's robes douses his hands in palm oil. The figure with the crown of chain and bone is led to a chair in the centre of the clearing. A minder pours oil over his head. Four men lift the calf to shoulder height. Another pulls its nostrils to bring the neck taut, and the last cuts its throat. The man in butcher's robes places his face under the cut. So much blood spills from the animal's neck that it overflows from his mouth.

My legs shake. Monsieur Antoine puts his hand again on my shoulder. He seems to be the only one in the crowd unmoved by the sacrifice. He continues to explain what is happening, his voice now carrying far across the silent crowd. The dancers, which he calls *the revenants* – the returning dead – were first brought to Benin from Oyo 200 years ago, by Yoruba prisoners of war. The organisation is very secret. It's forbidden to see below the cloths. If they come to a house for food, he says, the owner must leave what he is eating and depart. One may never watch them eat. When they bow down to talk, as some do now, they relate messages from the ancestors. Often, they are present at funerals. They process through the streets with drums, to ensure the dead reach the otherworld. They are part of grief.

When I read for the first time 'Dream Song #235', I remember thinking how common it seems for something buried deep in the past to stir again, years or decades later, and out of nowhere come back.

'Tears Henry shed for poor old Hemingway', John Berryman began 'Dream Song #235', 'Hemingway in despair, Hemingway at the end'. The poem ended, two verses later, with the narrator pleading with his father not to pull the trigger of a shotgun.

I knew little about Berryman's writing, nothing of his life. I went from the book to Wikipedia, where I followed Berryman's poem through wormhole after wormhole. Henry, I learned, who appears throughout Berryman's *Dream Songs*, was a character who'd suffered a terrible loss, and had a close resemblance to Berryman himself. Hemingway had killed himself with a shotgun in July 1961, in Ketchum, Idaho. Hemingway's father had shot himself thirty years before in Oak Park, Illinois.

On Berryman's biography page, I read that when he was eleven, his father woke early at the family home in Clearwater, Florida, and shot himself. Fifty years later Berryman threw himself from a Minneapolis bridge, onto the bank of the Mississippi River.

'I'm cross with god who has wrecked this generation,' Berryman began another Dream Song: 'First he seized Ted, then Richard, Randall, and now Delmore. In between he gorged on Sylvia Plath.' I followed Wikipedia on through the lives of those poets. How Randall

Jarrell sat for days crying in front of the television after JFK's assassination – 'sad to the point of inertia', according to his biographer – before being admitted to hospital, and soon after dying on a highway. How Delmore Schwartz died alone in the Chelsea Hotel, after years of deteriorating mental health. How Sylvia Plath, whose father, Otto, had died when she was eight, struggled and wrote, struggled and wrote, until the end; how her son Nicholas, a biologist who specialised in stream ecology, took his own life in Fairbanks, Alaska, five decades after his mother.

I don't know if I was drawn to these histories out of some macabre voyeurism, or because I thought they could teach me something about becoming a writer, or because I wanted to stoke something up inside myself. I had a sense, though, reading the stories of the lives of the poets in the *Dream Songs*, that life was like a boomerang, that the same wounds open and reopen, over and over.

Each time I attend a funeral the same feeling comes to me. The last I attended was for my uncle, who worked all his life as a foreign correspondent and died aged sixty-eight from a rare form of cancer. On a grey September day, cold and damp, our family gathered for the ceremony at a burial ground in Otford, Kent. We formed, on the path from the car park, a short procession behind the undertakers. My uncle had selected the burial ground as an alternative to a traditional cemetery. There, plots were marked with sapling trees.

I carried a handheld cassette player, on which played Feste's song from Shakespeare's *Twelfth Night*, sung by an actor with whom my uncle had been friends. I walked behind my mother, my aunt and cousins, and the priest.

The speakers were not powerful enough to carry the music fully, and the song was grainy in the air. When we reached my uncle's plot, on the edge of the field, we stood in silence, waiting for the song to end. The priest led the burial service from the Book of Common Prayer and we sang a hymn. As the service drew to an end, my aunt handed us each a sprig of rosemary – a reference to a line about remembrance in *Hamlet*, my aunt said – which we dropped, one by one, onto the coffin. It was then that my cousin began to sing. He sang alone, to no music, in Russian: a language he and my uncle spoke as they'd lived in Moscow for my uncle's work. I felt a familiar feeling well up as my cousin sang. I cried uncontrollably.

The same thing happens at each funeral I attend. When the music starts, I become overwhelmed. Even though I'm aware of what will come, the strength of the emotion shocks me. I try to hold myself together for the people around me, but I can never keep it in. I'm not conscious of thinking of my father during these moments, but it's the only source capable of drawing such a strong reaction.

Walking, I've thought back sometimes to those moments, as old feelings and memories that I didn't know were there have washed up in my steps. Now, nearing the end, I try to visualise whatever was painful from that time drifting out of me, scattering to the road behind.

12

On Good Friday, 1810, friar Don Bernardo Abeyta, standing in a New Mexico field, saw a light rising from a mountainside. The legend of Chimayo holds that Abeyta climbed to the light and dug by hand to uncover the source, finding a wooden cross in the earth. He built a chapel on the site. Today, two centuries on, tens of thousands of pilgrims travel each Holy Week to Chimayo.

'The walker toiling along a road toward some distant place is one of the most compelling and universal images of what it means to be human,' Rebecca Solnit wrote, reflecting on her own pilgrimage to Chimayo. Approaching the hills at Dassa, for the first time among other pilgrims, I get what Solnit means. Monsieur Antoine said I'd find more people at Dassa than I'd ever seen before in one place. Looking at the crowds of pilgrims on the road ahead, bundles on their heads, stretching to where the dusts blur the horizon, I see that he was right. Walking among them, I feel part of something.

The sun is low and the air glows yellow. Dust hangs at eye level. There are so many people the buses can only pass in one direction. Old women sit on the roofs, which are piled high with firewood and sacks of grain. On their heads, the pilgrims carry stoves, rugs, bags of rice. Some lead donkeys. Children hold hands in long chains.

Dassa-Zoumé is nothing like the image I had in my mind when I left Bawku. The mountains are rock outcrops more than mountains. They rise in rings around basin valleys, lumps of grey and black. Forests hang from them. Where the slopes are gentler, plantain and manioc grow. The town is a cluster of tin-roofed bungalows, crowded between the rocks. Across from the mountain, to which we walk, there's a vast market. The stalls sell plastic relics, neon rosaries, phials of holy water. Vendors have come from Lomé and Abidjan. They offer T-shirts of the Pope, Chinese toys, saints painted onto plastic clocks. The market has drawn all manner of faces. Herders have come to sell cattle, their wives to buy cloth. Girls dance in glittering veils, some with hi-fis on their shoulders. Orphans have journeyed from Cotonou and Porto Novo. Prostitutes stand outside makeshift bars. Men with leprosy sit at the basilica gates. In the basilica grounds, the pilgrims have tied laundry lines to the trees. Many have lit fires. The air smells of diesel, excrement, burning herbs. I follow the pilgrims through the smoke, to the base of the rocks, where we begin to climb.

At Chimayo, pilgrims are given holy dirt from the church Don Abeyta built. The pilgrims rub the earth on themselves in the hope it will purify them. At Dassa pilgrims perform the stations of the cross, which are marked on plaques set into the rock. The Ancient Greeks, who walked the Sacred Way to Eleusis, danced on the Rharian Field. Pilgrims to Kumbh Mela, the largest human gathering in the world, bathe where the rivers meet.

Zen teachers sometimes talk about *the circle of the way*. The idea of the circle, they say, is that you cannot separate the practice from the goal. The purpose is not to arrive, but to keep going. Seen this way, the ritual of the pilgrimage end can help give the journey meaning, but the power of pilgrimage is in the distance before. Buddhist and Zen pilgrimages often go in circles. Tendai monks who undertake the *kaihōgyō* run around the mountain day after day, for years. Pilgrims to Mount Kailash, which Buddhists, Hindus, Bonpos and Jains believe to be the centre of the earth, complete thirty-mile circumambulations of the mountain base. Walking around and around the mountain, there's no end or summit, just steps on a circuit that could go on forever.

The idea of the circle, those who travel to Kailash say, is to bring the pilgrim closer to a transcendent state. Nan Shepherd said she came to understand what drew the Buddhist pilgrim to the mountain, in the Cairngorms, the mountains to which she returned throughout her life. 'The journey is itself part of the technique by which god is sought,' Shepherd wrote.

> It is a journey into Being; for as I penetrate more deeply into the mountain's life, I penetrate also into my own. For an hour I am beyond desire. It is not ecstasy, that leap out of the self that makes man like a god. I am not out of myself, but in myself. I am. To know Being, this is the final grace accorded from the mountain.

Some of those who undertake the Kailash pilgrimage do so performing protestations, in which they kneel, stretch out and crawl around the mountain, in a ritual that leaves their hands and knees bleeding, and can take months. A number of those who walk to Chimayo each year do so barefoot. Some of the pilgrims on the road to Dassa drag heavy crosses. Struggle is part of any pilgrimage. Like sanding down a surface, the struggle helps the walker strip away the things that don't matter. With time, the idea is that the hardship breaks the person down, laying the ground for what they hope they'll reach at the journey's end: rebirth.

A few miles from Chimayo, in the town of Taos, New Mexico, as they looked up at the peaks of the Sangre de Cristo Mountains, the old Pueblo man asked Jung if he did not think that all life came from the mountain.

Thirty years earlier, as a teenager on a journey with his father to Vitznau, on Lake Lucerne, Jung's father had bought him a ticket for the mountain railway which went from the lake to the summit of Mount Rigi. Jung recalled being awe-struck as he hiked the mountain paths in the cold, thin air. He felt, he said, that he was in God's world. Later, Jung remembered the Rigi railway ticket as the most precious gift his father had ever given him.

Reflecting on the question posed by the old Pueblo man three decades after Rigi, Jung watched the river flow from the peaks of the Sangre de Cristo Mountains, bringing water into the world, and it struck him that nothing could be more obvious than the mountain as the source of life. He remembered then what he described as 'a swelling emotion' on just hearing the word mountain. It was as if, as a place and an idea, the mountain had retained the power he'd first experienced on Rigi, all those years before.

At around that time, Jung had bought a property in the village of Bollingen, on the shore of Lake Zurich. There, he worked to restore the old stone building, which had fallen into disrepair. He built by hand a stone tower, carving the grey rocks with a hammer and chisel. He retreated to Bollingen for weeks on end, living in a way that was little different to his ancestors centuries before. 'I have done without electricity,' he wrote, 'and tend the fireplace and stove myself. Evenings, I light the old lamps. There is no running water, and I pump the water from the well. I chop the wood and cook the food.'

Jung believed his way of life at Bollingen, and the atmosphere he'd created in the house, helped sustain the souls of his ancestors. He spoke sometimes of humans being made up of two parts. The first part, he said, was the person who'd lived the years since they were born; the second was a more ancient being, which went right back to the first peoples, to the Taung Child and Langebaan Eve. He believed the human mind was formed of consciousness from both. At its deepest root, Jung visualised the oldest strata of the psyche, which had evolved over millions of years, as naked bedrock.

Jung seemed to have made the process of building his stone tower, in some way at least, a commemoration of those who'd passed. He built the first tower at Bollingen shortly after the death of his mother. Thirty years later, after the death of his wife, Emma, Jung added a second storey to one of the towers he'd first restored in the 1920s. He described drawing his ancestors on the walls. 'It is as if a silent, greater family', he wrote, 'stretching down the centuries, were peopling the house'.

Pilgrims sometimes describe their journeys as generating this kind of remembering: the daily struggle of the steps draws out connections with the past. Part of this, I think, is the quiet that comes with doing one thing at a time. The day is made up of one step after another, a few basic tasks. I am only ever walking, filling my bottles, preparing food, making up or taking down my camp. The days hang together without thought, bound loosely by an idea that rarely surfaces, but is there: that putting one foot in front of the other can change your life.

The result of having so few inputs is a kind of clearing. I feel this as I settle to the pace of those ahead, climbing the final stretch up the Dassa mountainside, no longer taking the steps fully consciously. My mind lets go of what's not necessary. Thoughts untangle and drift to the surface. When pilgrims talk about walking and remembering, I think they are describing this opening of space, which fills with memories that needed to come back.

# Sea

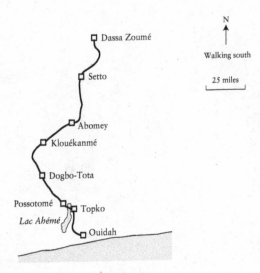

*From Dassa-Zoumé to Ouidah, a former slave port on the Atlantic coast; 130 miles through the old kingdom of Dahomey, once one of the most powerful states in West Africa. The route follows a mix of road and track, via Abomey, the old Dahomean capital, and the fishing community Possotomé, on the shores of Lac Ahémé.*

# I

The chief sits alone by the tracks. I sit on my pack beside him. We sit this way for three hours, talking barely. After a long silence, the chief gets up. I follow him to the road, where a minibus has pulled in. He supervises the load of sacks onto the roof, groundnuts he's sending to sell in Cotonou. We watch the bus disappear into the dust.

The chief walks slowly, with a cane, as we make our way across the tracks towards his compound. He was born in Parakou, he says, but came to work the railroad as a teenager and never left. He's been in Setto sixty years. The village has 5,000 residents, he says; each he knows by name.

Setto is a highway village, on the main road, twenty-five miles south of Dassa, 120 miles north of Ouidah. Stalls line the verge: cauldrons of soup; bundles of cloth; petrol in Pastis bottles. People lead donkeys from the hills loaded with crop. On the corners, women peel oranges with razor blades.

The chief lights a lamp. His son brings us each a baguette with a bowl of condensed milk. It's Ramadan, and the chief breaks the fast this way each night. He lays a straw mat on the floor. I roll my clothes into a pillow, bundled in my scarf, and arrange my things for the morning. I tear a page from my journal and write a note to thank him. I lie awake in the dark a while. Hours later I hear a woman groaning across the room. The hut door is shut, and the air is close. I wake to grey light seeping through the walls. The chief is asleep, and the other body is gone. I gather my things and roll up the mat. I leave the note on the table, and make my way back across the tracks to the road.

The rain is misty. At the Dan junction, where the tracks split, I take the red road via Samadjagon. Palms rise from the fields. In the villages there are straw churches painted with rainbows. Tyres and rocks are on the roofs to stop the metal sheets blowing away.

The maize stubble is burning on the outskirts of Abomey. The rain falls heavily. It subdues the flames and puddles spread across the mud. Children huddle beneath the awnings, looking out through smoky air. The sky is so dark the stallholders light their lamps. I pass a palace, a long red-walled compound, built, it says on a plaque, by Akaba, Dahomey's second king. Fire destroyed many of the city's palaces, after Béhanzin set light to the city as the French advanced. A second wave of flames, fanned by Harmattan winds, burned down the refurbished palaces a century later.

The rainbow spirit settled in Abomey the year the great famine ended – 1721 – says the priest at the temple in the Dètohou quarter. The priest, who I visit on my first morning in the city, sleeps in his shrine, surrounded by the statues he tends. He rises at 4.30 each morning to give the spirits water, a rite his father – who died aged 112 – performed before him for sixty years.

There are rainbows, too, on the walls of Mouriatou's temple, west of the city. Mouriatou, a priestess of the sea goddess Mami Wata, wears a white sheet and has a tattoo of a chameleon on her arm. Trainee priests sit in silence outside the shrine houses, many of which are painted with murals: of snakes, rainbows, three-headed figures with yellow skin and red spots. The priests wear red cloth and have wooden dolls tucked into their robes.

Mami Wata emerged in West Africa in the nineteenth century as old and settled ways of life fell apart in the face of colonial occupation. She has roots in ancient Egypt as Mami Uati, a figure of Isis; in Babylon as Mami Aruru; in Mesopotamia as Ninhursag, the Lady of the Sacred Mountain. She came to West Africa in fragments: on parchments carried by desert mystics, as mermaids engraved on the bows of Portuguese ships, on scraps of holy texts brought by Indian merchants. She comes from the sea to people in their dreams when they are struggling, Mouriatou says. She brings rebirth.

A wide, red piste runs south from Abomey across the plateau. It's the type of road that in summer would throw up choking dust, where only the outline of the palms, the scooters, the figures with brushwood would be visible. In rainy season the road would be impassable. The mud would clag, and water would fill the trenches. Now, the rains have dried out. The earth is hard-packed and there's no dust. The road has spring, and the surface is even, which makes it steady to walk. It cuts straight across the plateau, so I can see far into the distance, which pulls me forward. The land is like this all the way to sea: a low plateau of red clay, swamps and cornfields.

I imagine what I will do when I reach Ouidah. I'll find a guesthouse, a small place with three or four rooms, somewhere with coffee, a bed with sheets, a shower. I'll do my stretches and press-ups. Then I'll find a place to write. I picture somewhere near the water, with shaded tables and cold beer. At the start of the walk, I wrote only basic notes at the end of each day. In each entry I noted the date, where I'd walked, how far I'd come, the weather, the village names. Often I wrote verbatim from what I'd spoken into my Dictaphone. I wanted to get something down to feel that the days were connected, to dispel the feeling that the miles were disappearing to nothing behind me.

Writing gradually became a daily practice. As I walked further, I wrote longer notes. Some days I manage only a few nothing sentences. On others, I fill the pages quickly. I feel during these spells like I sometimes feel on the road. I have so much energy that if I stop to speak or to adjust something, my legs shake, and I have to rub my hands together to give the energy somewhere to go.

As I come closer to the end, I have a sense that I'm being pulled in. I drive my steps harder, so the stick comes to the ground at a faster tempo, and my breath shortens. I stop infrequently. When I stop, I do no more than refill my bottles and douse my head in water. I eat as I move. I hold onto the shoulder strap of my pack, as if I might break into a run. I create sums in my mind with the distance left, rolling the miles together to work out the number of hours to go if I continued through the night without stopping.

Sixty miles north of Ouidah, I take a room in a bar at Klouékanmé. A man with no legs dances on his hands. Men throw coins and bottle tops at him. The barman shows me a room in the back. He switches on the light, which flickers as if the bulb might blow. There's a foam mattress and a bucket. Crates are stacked in the corner and there are cockroaches on the floor. I try to sleep, but the noise from the bar goes late. Drinkers come in looking for somewhere to piss. I set up my tent to keep out the mosquitoes. I write with my head torch in the tent in the room.

From Klouékanmé, the track climbs over gentle hills and falls into sinks of brown water. Power lines sway in the wind. Machetes rise above the grass tops, the farm children who hold them hidden. Birds fly from swamp apple trees. Biting flies collect at my calves and shoulders. I whip my scarf over my legs and back. Sometimes I take the wrong path and a man at the end of the track leads me back. I walk this way for two days, zigzagging on paths through the swamps.

It's close to dusk when I reach Possotomé, on the shore of Lac Ahémé. Tumbledown huts give onto the water. The sun glows between the palms. Men smoke fish on fires in the sand. Children sit in circles around baskets of fighting crabs. Women gut tilapia in the yards. Canoes are pulled up between the trees. Villagers gather as the boats come in.

I meet Adam on the beach. He wears blue wayfarers and sits alone beneath a tree. Travellers sometimes come to the village, and Adam has set himself up as a guide. He takes me on a tour, showing me the best fishing spots, the forests and the temples. He asks if I'll go to his house for food.

Marie, Adam's wife, cooks on a stove in the yard. They live in a mud-walled house on the far side of the village from the lake. Oil spits from the pan. Marie's face is marked with scars, and she has a baby on her back. We eat on deck chairs over a plank of wood balanced on two bricks. The mats they sleep on are rolled up against the wall.

Marie's opening a salon, Adam says. They can get the best lotions from people he knows in Cotonou: at a good price. Things that people here haven't seen before. They'll fit the place out simply, he says, but with style, so people will pass and see it's a good place.

Marie brings more food: maize and fish heads in red sauce. The surrounding huts are close, and the clinking of pans and shouting is constant. A gust of wind blows the door and the lamp flame dies.

Each month they put a little money aside, Adam says. In six months, seven at most, they'll have enough. As we eat, they tell all the details of how it will be. They'll have the best lotions and nice pictures on the walls, so people feel that it's a good place; how word will spread and customers will travel just for the salon. It will be by the lake, Marie says, close to the water where people will want to sit a while. They nod as they speak, as if they're really talking to each other, reassuring themselves that this is how it will be.

The palms are still at dawn. The men arrange their nets and push the boats into the water. It's 5.30. I get into a canoe, which rocks unsteadily. The fisherman uses a bamboo punt. Every few minutes we stop and bail water from the bottom of the canoe. Looking back to the shore, I see figures on the beach, fires being lit. In the water between, there are white flags tethered to stakes, and the tips of tall reeds. Men cast nets in the mist.

On the far bank, the fisherman points to roofs beyond the trees. Topko, he says. I put on my pack and walk for the village. I buy bananas and groundnuts. A dust road goes south to Ouidah, which is seventeen miles away.

The mud is dry here, the colour of rust. In places the vegetation has been cut back and there are shrines to Legba beneath corrugated shelters. Stray dogs rest beneath the trees. Old men sit on chairs beside them. Reeds rise from the shallows. Children wheel bicycles into the lake to wash away the dust.

Most of the past five months I've spent on dirt roads like this. Each day I've followed the same routine. I've woken at five. My first task is to dismantle the tent. I brush down the groundsheet, collapse the poles, load it into my pack. I'm on the road at 5.30, as the sky begins to grey. The first hours of the day were the hours I liked best. I walked for seven, twelve, sometimes sixteen hours. I stopped for food, water, shade. I progressed slowly.

It took time to adapt. The first struggle was to accept that each day I was walking, with nothing else. Everything from before had been stripped away, like waking up in a new world. I had to shed impulses which had built up over years.

Each night I got in, I rinsed my clothes, set my tent, filled my bottles. Before I left home, I thought carrying little would be restrictive. But I came to see it as freeing. Walking in the desert, camping off the road, taking care of my feet and my food each evening, that became my whole life.

Sometimes I woke in nightmarish places: camping miles from shelter in a storm, alone in the rain and the lithium light; or a mattress on a floor with cockroaches and rats. The sores on my hands and thighs stung as I came awake. My skin was tight from the sun. My stomach churned. I could lie back, eyes closed for a few more minutes, or get up and walk. The only thing to do was to walk.

Sometimes I walked until I was numb, too tired to form my steps properly, to think. I blacked out. At times the monotony was overwhelming: all I felt was anger. I saw the walk as a fight in those moments. I imagined each time

I didn't give in would make me stronger. I needed the struggle to help me make sense.

As the miles built up behind me, I felt release, that I was beginning to face the sadness which I'd held since my earliest memories.

It's hot now. For the first day in many, the sky is clear. The sun is white. I walk on the edge of the track, beside men going to the fields and women with cans of water on their heads. The road passes groves of palms and reeds. The wind blows through the trees. Dust drifts across the track.

I have the same daydream I often have. I'm one of a band of people that has survived a disaster. We've settled an abandoned village. We've sown fields to grow food and dug a well. We've fixed up houses and have trees for firewood. Over the years the land has turned dusty and the well has become low. A river runs a few miles from the settlement. We decide to dig a trench to bring water. Each day I travel to the end of the trench and dig. Each night I come back, and the water is a little closer. I'm knee-deep in the water, packing down wet mud to form the walls. I drive stakes into the sides to keep them from collapsing. Eels come from the mud. I work through the distance we cover each day in my mind as I walk. We start with four kilometres to dig. After two months we've dug half of it. Each day we dig another segment: thirty metres a day. I add up the days and the distance in my mind as I walk, and the water gets closer. Others start to dig from the village side. I always snap from the daydream before the trenches join and the water floods to the end pool. The dream is a kind of mental game. It makes visible the idea that my steps add up to something.

*

The houses on the outskirts of Ouidah are orange and rose pink. Worn shutters shelter glassless windows. The paint has peeled from the wood in the heat. Hanging gardens drop from the porticos. Above the doorways there are plaques marked with the household name. Children play boules with crushed cans filled with sand. Rubbish collectors pass with rickshaws.

I follow a dirt road to the square of the Basilica of the Immaculate Conception. A man with a python stands across from the church gates. *C'est magnifique, notre église*, he says. He wears a blue suit, has ten scars on his face, and shows the snake to a tourist.

The road comes out at Place Chacha. In the centre of the square there's a tree draped in the flags of Caribbean and American countries to which slaves were sent. The wind blows hot from the lagoon. The shore is two miles down a sand track. The sand goes red to white. I pass the village of Zoungbodji. The houses are whitewashed with oyster lime. A sheet has been drawn around the trunk of the largest tree. Beside it a goat skull is nailed to a post. Those sold into slavery were said to have walked around two trees in the village: the Tree of Forgetting, which they circled in a ritual designed to rid them of their past identities; and the Tree of Return, which they passed to help their souls find a way home after death.

A bridge crosses the lagoon. Baskets are laid to trap the salt, where stilt houses stand in the marshes. Palms rise from the far side of the water. The track comes over a rise, down to the beach. On the shore, metal figures bound to one another flank a gate. A mural shows slaves being led to the sea. Beside it, there's a statue of an *egungun* and a plaque which says *Door of No Return* in gold. A cross of polished stone stands beside the memorial.

A wide beach of yellow sand drops to the water. The sea is rough and the wind brings spray from the waves. The salt stings my eyes. Crabs run from the sand. In both directions I can see the beach all the way until the horizon disappears. Cattle walk at the water's edge.

I remember during my last day of work at the law firm, the head of my department said a few words in the open area beside our desks. It was a set of words I'd heard many times as colleagues moved on, but as I stood with my card, surrounded by the other lawyers, I felt a sense of loss. The feeling grew as I gathered my belongings from the room I rented in my friend's house. It was uncomfortable to be back, a few hours later, in my childhood room in Oxford.

I lived for a week at home in Oxford before I flew to Accra. I'd planned to be busy with final preparations for the journey, but there was little to do by then. Things surfaced from the room – old clothes, movie posters, my father's books – which drew me back to a different time. Among those objects I had a feeling of being on an edge which I could no longer back away from. The feeling grew each day until I walked to the bus station with my rucksack. Walking the road from Dassa-Zoumé to Ouidah, I felt the same sensation: that each day I got closer, I was nearing a precipice. Now I'm here, the anxiety that came back as I neared the end – the returning awareness that I have no job, no house, no money – has melted away. Those things are the future. The walk, I see now, was always about the past.

I remember the long stretch of sand on the beach at St Andrews, looking out to the North Sea. My grandfather always walked to the same section of that beach, in the shelter of the dunes. He spent time selecting the best place to build his sandcastle. I was never sure why he delayed, but I think now that he was balancing in his mind the consistency of the sand, the degree to which the place was sheltered by the wind, and the distance from the tide.

He measured carefully the layout of the castle, drawing on his pipe as he marked the plan in the sand. My brother and I walked beside him, impatient to begin. He had a meticulous way of digging, which yielded a moat with walls at a steady angle and an even depth. We dug alongside him, creating a great mound within the moat. We patted down the sides of the walls and, where we needed more sand, shuttled from a pit we dug further off. My grandfather worked on the most intricate features of the castle, only over the years slowly entrusting bits of this to us. He fashioned from the sand spherical turrets, into which he cut crenellations. With his trowel he drew crosses on the turret sides. He dug steps into the smoothed walls which went from the drawbridge to the castle high point. When he had dug several steps, setting an even width and depth, he allowed us to build, watching over our efforts with his pipe and, afterwards, carefully smoothing with his trowel any we had carved too hastily. As the tide came in, we stood back and watched the sea fill the moat, then pull away the walls.

As our grandfather got older, he struggled to stoop down, which meant he couldn't get close enough to the walls to build the steps himself or to mark the crosses on the turrets. He lowered himself as far as he could, his pipe in his mouth and his white hair blowing in the wind, instructing us where to add more sand and which places to smooth out. At some point he could no longer cross the dunes on foot, and we wheeled him in a chair to sit in the bandstand, a thick rug across his lap. He struggled to hear then, and he leaned close to us, trying to pick the words from the wind that blew over the cliffs, as he asked about the castles on the beach below.

I wondered later what he was teaching us with his sandcastles. I used to think that he found in them some outlet for his mathematical mind; that, as in a game of chess, he took pleasure in the process of getting the angles correct, the grains to stand together in the order he sought. When the sea came in, I stared at my grandfather, watching for his reaction as the castle collapsed into the frothy water. He stared impassively, pipe in hand. I think he was teaching us that, although the sea will come in, it's still worthwhile work.

# Acknowledgements

Many people along the walk gave me guidance and help, countless meals, safe places to sleep, company. I would never have made it without them. Thank you to each of them, and to the many others who shared ideas and took time to teach me things. Special thanks to Auntie in Accra, to Beatrice and Blessing in Kade, to Nana Abass in Kumasi, to the monks at Tanoboase, to Prince and his family in Dawadawa, to Adupukari in Pigu, to Ernest in Tengzug, to the people who cared for me in Dapaong, to Larry in Barkoisi, to Antoine and Armand in Savalou, to Marc in Abomey, to Adam and Marie in Possotomé, and to Francis in Ouidah.

Back home, thanks to my family, and to Alice, for their patience and support with me writing; to my friend Katie and my cousin Al, who read early edits and gave me guidance; and to my agent Chris, and my editor Bea, and Daisy from her team, who believed in the idea, and taught me so much about writing.

# Bibliography

## Forest

Geoffrey Parrinder, *West African Religion* (London: The Epworth Press, 1949), 22, 58, 153–5, 170

John Parker, *Making the Town: Ga State and Society in Early Colonial Accra* (Oxford: James Currey, 2000), 6

Ben Okri, *The Famished Road* (London: Jonathan Cape, 1991)

Henry David Thoreau, *Walden and Civil Disobedience* (New York: Penguin Books, 1986, first published 1854), 46

Margaret M. Hansen, Reo Jones and Kirsten Tocchini (2017), 'Shinrin-Yoku (Forest Bathing) and Nature Therapy: A State-of-the-Art Review', *International Journal of Environmental Research and Public Health*, 14(8), 851

Bum Jin Park et al. (2010), 'Physiological effects of Forest Recreation in a Young Conifer Forest in Hinokage Town, Japan', *Silva Fennica*, 43(2): 291–301

Bum Jin Park et al. (2010), 'The physiological effects of Shinrin-yoku (taking in the forest atmosphere or forest bathing): evidence from field experiments in 24 forests across Japan', *Journal of Environmental Health and Preventive Medicine*, 15(1):18–26

Juyoung Lee et al. 'Nature Therapy and Preventive Medicine', in Jay Maddock, ed., *Public Health, Social and Behavioral Health* (Rijeka: InTech, 2012), chapter 16

Bum Jin Park et al. (2007), 'Physiological effects of Shinrin-yoku (taking in the atmosphere of the forest): using salivary cortisol and cerebral activity as indicators', *Journal of Physiological Anthropology*, 26. 123–8. 10.2114

Yuki Ideno et al. (2017), 'Blood pressure-lowering effect of Shinrin-yoku (Forest bathing): a systematic review and meta-analysis', *BMC Complementary and Alternative Medicine*, 16;17(1):409

Qing Li et al. (2011), 'Acute effects of walking in forest environments on cardiovascular and metabolic parameters', *European Journal of Applied Physiology*, 111; 2845–2853

Gwang-Won Kim et al. (2010), 'Functional neuroanatomy associated with natural and urban scenic views in the human brain: 3.0T functional MR imaging', *Korean Journal of Radiology*, 11(5):507–13

Roger Ulrich (1984), 'View through a window may influence recovery from surgery', *Science*, 224, 420(2)

Florence Williams, *The Nature Fix: Why Nature Makes Us Happier, Healthier, and More Creative* (New York: W.W. Norton & Company, 2017)

John Muir, *John of the Mountains: The Unpublished Journals of John Muir*, ed. Linnie Marsh Wolfe (Madison: The University of Wisconsin Press, 1966, first published 1938), 313, 429

Richard Taylor et al. (2017), 'The Implications of Fractal Fluency for Biophilic Architecture', *Journal of Biourbanism*, 6, 23–40

Richard Taylor and Branka Spehar, 'Fractal Fluency: An Intimate Relationship Between the Brain and Processing of

Fractal Stimuli', in Antonio Di Leva, ed., *The Fractal Geometry of the Brain* (Berlin: Springer, 2016)

Caroline Hagerhall (2008), 'Investigations of human EEG response to viewing fractal patterns', *Perception*, 37, 1488–1494

Ludovic Ferrière, Christian Koeberl and Wolf Uwe Reimold (2010) 'Drill core LB-08A, Bosumtwi impact structure, Ghana: Petrographic and shock metamorphic studies of material from the central uplift', *Meteoritics & Planetary Science*, 42, 611–633

Christian Koeberl et al. (2007), 'An international and multi-disciplinary drilling project into a young complex impact structure' *Meteoritics and Planetary Science*, 42, 483–511

'Lake Bosomtwe' https://sites.google.com/site/ghanaplace-names/places-in-perspective/bosomtwe

Harvey M. Feinberg (1989), 'Africans and Europeans in West Africa: Elminans and Dutchmen on the Gold Coast During the Eighteenth Century' *Transactions of the American Philosophical Society*, 79(7), 25–44

Kwame Arhin (1978), 'Gold-mining and trading among the Ashanti of Ghana' *Journal des Africanistes*, 48(1), 89–100

'The Trans-Saharan Gold Trade (7th–14th Century)', in *Heilbrunn Timeline of Art History, Department of the Arts of Africa, Oceania, and the Americas*, The Metropolitan Museum of Art, New York (October 2000) http://www.metmuseum.org/toah/hd/gold/hd_gold.htm

Paul Lovejoy, *Transformations in Slavery: A History of Slavery in Africa* (Cambridge: Cambridge University Press, 1983), 46–63

Kwamina Dickson, *A Historical Geography of Ghana* (Cambridge: Cambridge University Press, 1969)

Harold Raugh, *The Victorians at War, 1815–1914: an Encyclopedia of British Military History* (Santa Barbara: ABC-CLIO, 2004)

Robert Edgerton, *The Fall of the Asante Empire: The Hundred-Year War for Africa's Gold Coast* (New York: Simon & Schuster, 1995)

'Asante', in *The Story of Africa, BBC World Service* http://www.bbc.co.uk/worldservice/specials/1624_story_of_africa/page85.shtml

Linda Lear, *Rachel Carson, Witness for Nature* (Boston: Mariner Books, 2009), 8

Rachel Carson, *The Sense of Wonder* (London: Harper & Row, 1965), 56

Stanley Temple (2015), 'Rachel Carson and a Childhood Sense of Wonder', *Wisconsin Academy Magazine* https://www.wisconsinacademy.org/magazine/rachel-carson-and-childhood-sense-wonder

Kathleen M. Trauth, Stephen C. Hora, and Robert V. Guzowski, 'Expert Judgment on Markers to Deter Inadvertent Human Intrusion into the Waste Isolation Pilot Plant', issued by *Sandia National Laboratory* for the United States Department of Energy (1993)

James Gerstenzang (14 May 1998), 'U.S. Approves 1st Permanent Tomb for Atomic Waste', *LA Times*, https://www.latimes.com/archives/la-xpm-1998-may-14-mn-49641-story.html

Thomas Sebeok, 'Communication Measures to Bridge Ten Millennia', *Technical Report prepared for the Office of Nuclear Waste Isolation* (1984)

Iégor Reznikoff (2012), 'On the Sound Related to Painted Caves and Rocks', in Janne Ikäheimo, Anna-Kaisa Salmi and Tiina Äikäs, eds., *Sounds Like Theory. XII Nordic Theoretical Archaeology Group Meeting in Oulu,*

*Monographs of the Archaeological Society of Finland,* 2, 101–09

Michael Rappenglück (2004), 'A Palaeolithic Planetarium Underground – the Cave of Lascaux (Part 1)' *Migration & Diffusion,* 5(18)

Bruno Fazenda et al. (2017), 'Cave acoustics in prehistory: Exploring the association of Palaeolithic visual motifs and acoustic response', *The Journal of the Acoustical Society of America,* 142(3)

Wade Davis, *The Wayfinders* (Toronto: House of Anansi Press, 2009), 26, 27–31, 122–3

Emilie Chalmin et al. (2006), 'Discovery of Unusual Minerals in Paleolithic Black Pigments from Lascaux (France) and Ekain (Spain)', *AIP Conference Proceedings* 882 pp. 220–22

Clayton Eshleman, *Juniper Fuse* (Middletown: Wesleyan University Press, 2003)

'Lakewood Community History', *LA County Library* https://lacountylibrary.org/lakewood-local-history/

D.J. Waldie, *Holy Land* (New York: W.W. Norton & Company, 1996), introduction v–vi, 11

'John E Martineau', *Eagle Tribune,* 29 November 2015, http://obituaries.eagletribune.com/obituary/john-martineau-771130911

'John Robert Martineau', *The Gazette,* 23 August 2016, https://www.legacy.com/obituaries/name/john-martineau-obituary?pid=181158671

'John Allen Martineau', *Johnson-Gloschat Funeral Home,* https://www.jgfuneralhome.com/tributes/John-Martineau

'Major Alfred John Martineau', *Sussex People,* http://www.sussexpeople.co.uk/major-alfred-john-martineau/

Tom McCaskie (2008), '"Akwantemfi" – "In Mid-Journey": an Asante Shrine Today and its Clients', *Journal of Religion in Africa,* 38, 57–80

Erika Bourguignon, *A Cross-Cultural Study of Dissociational States* (Columbus: Ohio State University Research Foundation, 1968), 11

Dharmavidya David Brazier, 'Pure and Simple Practice', *Tricycle*, Winter (2018),
https://tricycle.org/magazine/nembutsu-pure-land-chant/

Mara Kelly (2009), 'The Ritual Path of Initiation into the Eleusinian Mysteries', *Rosicrucian Digest*, No. 2

Simon Hornblower, Antony Spawforth and Esther Eidinow, 'The Oxford Classical Dictionary' (Oxford: Oxford University Press, 2012)

Dudley Wright, *The Eleusinian Mysteries and Rites* (London: The Theosophical Publishing House, 1919)

Joshua Mark, 'The Eleusinian Mysteries: The Rites of Demeter', *Ancient History Encyclopedia* (January 2012) https://www.ancient.eu/article/32/the-eleusinian-mysteries-the-rites-of-demeter/

Jan Bremmer, *Initiation into the Mysteries of the Ancient World* (Boston: Walter de Gruyter, 2014), 1–16

R. Gordon Wasson, Albert Hofmann, and Carl Ruck, *The Road to Eleusis: Unveiling the Secret of the Mysteries* (Berkeley: North Atlantic Books, 2008)

Marius Tullius Cicero, *On the Republic, on the Laws,* trans. Clinton W. Keyes (Cambridge: Harvard University Press, 1928, first published circa 51 BCE), Laws II xiv, 36

Bruce Chatwin, *Songlines* (London: Penguin Books, 1987)

Lama Anagarika Govinda, *The Way of the White Clouds* (London: Rider & Co, 1966), 78, 91

Robert Rhodes (1987), 'The Kaihogyo Practice of Mt. Hiei', *Japanese Journal of Religious Studies*, 14, 2–3

Rebecca Solnit, *Wanderlust* (London: Verso, 2001), 5, 30, 50

Michael Winkelman 'The Integrative Mode of Consciousness: Evolutionary Origins of Ecstasy', in Torsten Passie,

Wilfried Belschner, Elisabeth Petrow eds. Würzburg Germany, *Ekstasen: Kontexte – Formen – Wirkungen* (Baden-Baden: Ergon-Verlag 2013), (English transcript: https://www.academia.edu/4165423/The_Integrative_Mode_of_Consciousness_Evolutionary_Origins_of_Ecstasy)

Phillip Sherotov and Chelsey Peat (2018), 'Your Brain on Altered States: on the Origin of Altering Consciousness', *Brain World,* https://brainworldmagazine.com/brain-altered-states-origin-altering-consciousness/1/

Nathaniel Kleitman, *Sleep and Wakefulness* (Chicago: University of Chicago Press, 1963)

Ruth Herbert, *Everyday Music Listening: Absorption, Dissociation and Trancing* (Farnham: Ashgate, 2011), 202–4

Mark Nelson, *Pushing our Limits: Insights from Biosphere 2* (Tuscon: The University of Arizona Press, 2018)

Tim Smit, *The Lost Gardens of Heligan* (London: Victor Gollancz, 1997)

Vasily Peskov, *Lost in the Taiga*, trans. Marian Schwartz (New York: Doubleday, 1994), 3–5, 43, 49–60, 72, 84–7, 176

Mike Dash (2013), 'For 40 Years, This Russian Family Was Cut Off From All Human Contact, Unaware of World War II', *Smithsonian Magazine*, https://www.smithsonianmag.com/history/for-40-years-this-russian-family-was-cut-off-from-all-human-contact-unaware-of-world-war-ii-7354256/

John Martin (2013), 'Meet the Last Lykov', *Vice Magazine*, https://www.vice.com/en_uk/article/dp4mzj/meet-the-last-lykov-000001-v20n4

Lucan, *Pharsalia III*, ed. and trans. Robert Graves (London: Penguin, 1956), 78–9, lines 399–453

Tacitus, *Annals*, ed. and trans. Michael Grant (London: Penguin, 1956), book 13 [40]

Both Lucan and Tacitus quoted in Carole Cusack, *The Sacred Tree: Ancient and Medieval Manifestations* (Newcastle: Cambridge Scholars Publishing, 2011), 63–70

Robert Bevan-Jones, *The Ancient Yew: a History of Taxus Baccata* (Oxford: Windgather Press, 2017), 128–9

Gary Varner, *The Mythic Forest, the Green Man and the Spirit of Nature* (New York: Algora Publishing, 2006)

'Gog & Magog' (2008) https://www.unitythroughdiversity. org/gog-magog.html

Melissa Leach and James Fairhead (2000), 'Challenging Neo-Malthusian Deforestation Analyses in West Africa's Dynamic Forest Landscapes', *Population and Development Review*, 26(1), 17–43, p. 19

Judy Ogutu, 'Can it be stopped? Ghana's forests "could completely disappear in 25 years"', *Mongabay* (August 2014) https://news.mongabay.com/2014/08/can-it-be-stopped-ghanas-forests-could-completely-disappear-in-less-than-25-years/

Farid ud-Din Attar, *The Conference of the Birds*, trans. Afkahm Darbandi and Dick Davis (London: Penguin, 1984)

'Kristo Buase Monastery', http://www.kristobuasemonastery.org/about

Frédéric Gros, *A Philosophy of Walking* (London: Verso, 2014), 9

Desert

Antoine de Saint-Exupéry, *The Little Prince*, trans. Irene Testot-Ferry (London: William Heineman, 1945), 73

Antoine de Saint-Exupéry, *Wind, Sand and Stars*, trans. Lewis Galantière (New York: Harcourt Brace & Company, 1967, first published 1939)

Bryan Swopes (29 December 2018), '29 December 1935: Wind, Sand and Stars', *This Day in Aviation*, https://www.thisdayinaviation.com/30-december-1935-wind-sand-stars/

Martin Buckley (20 July 2004), 'The Other Side of the Story', *The Telegraph*, https://www.telegraph.co.uk/culture/3621040/The-other-side-of-the-story.html

Peter deMenocal and Jessica Tierney (2012), 'Green Sahara: African Humid Periods Paced by Earth's Orbital Changes', *Nature Education Knowledge* 3(10): 12

Joanna Casey, 'Just a Formality: The Presence of Fancy Projectile Points in a Basic Tool Assemblage', in Susan Kent, ed., *Gender in African Pre-History* (London: Altamira, 1998), 83–103

'Archaeological Sites and other sites of historical-cultural relevance to Ghana', http://www.ghanamuseums.org/archaeo-sites-others.php

Joanna Casey, 'The Stone to Metal Age in West Africa', in Peter Mitchell and Paul Lane, eds., *The Oxford Handbook of African Archaeology* (Oxford: Oxford University Press, 2013), 603–14

Catherine D'Andrea and Joanna Casey (2002), 'Pearl Millet and Kintampo Subsistence', in *African Archaeological Review* 19(3): 147–173

Graeme Barker, *The Agricultural Revolution in Prehistory: Why did Foragers become Farmers* (Oxford: Oxford University Press, 2006)

Gordon Childe, *The Most Ancient East: The Oriental Prelude to European Prehistory* (London: Kegan Paul, 1929)

Melinda Zeder (2011), 'The Origins of Agriculture in the Near East', *Current Anthropology*, 52(4), S221–S235

Michael Balter (2005), 'The Seeds of Civilization', *Smithsonian Magazine*, https://www.smithsonianmag.com/history/the-seeds-of-civilization-78015429/

Jacques Chauvin, *The Birth of the Gods and the Origins of Agriculture*, trans. Trevor Watkins (Cambridge: Cambridge University Press, 2000)

Melinda Zeder (2011), 'Religion and the Revolution: the Legacy of Jacques Chauvin', *Paléorient*, 37(1), 36–60
https://www.persee.fr/doc/paleo_0153-9345_2011_num_37_1_5437

Annette Kobak, *Isabelle: the Life of Isabelle Eberhardt* (New York: Vintage, 1990), 17, 33, 35, 107, 227

Emma Garman, 'Feminize Your Canon: Isabelle Eberhardt', *The Paris Review* (February 2019), https://www.theparisreview.org/blog/2019/02/11/feminize-your-canon-isabelle-eberhardt/

Paul Bowles, 'Baptism of Solitude', in *Their Heads are Green and their Hands are Blue* (London: Harper Perennial, 2006), 134

Syrine Hout (2000), 'Grains of Utopia: The Desert as Literary Oasis in Paul Bowles' *The Sheltering Sky* and Wilfred Thesiger's *Arabian Sands*', *Utopian Studies*, 11(2), 112–36

Edith Bone, *Seven Years Solitary* (London: Hamish Hamilton, 1957), 78, 80, 81, 89, 93–4, 97, 99–101

Stephen Belcher, *African Myths of Origin* (London: Penguin, 2005), 54–5

Anthony Hamilton Millard Kirk-Greene, '*Maudu Laawol Pulaaku*: survival and symbiosis', in Mahidi Adamu and Anthony Hamilton Millard Kirk-Greene, eds., *Pastoralists of the West Africa Savanna* (Manchester: Manchester University Press, 1979), 40–54

'Fulani Initiation Rites', *National Geographic*, https://video.nationalgeographic.com/video/00000144-0a42-d3cb-a96c-7b4f54370000

'Tassili n'Ajjer', *Unesco*, https://whc.unesco.org/en/list/179

Amadou Hampaté Ba and Germaine Dieterlen (1966), 'Les fresques d'époque bovidienne du Tassili N'Ajjer et les traditions des Peul: hypothèses d'interprétation', in *Journal de la Société des Africanistes*, 36(1), 141–57

Yaa Oppong, *Moving through and passing on: Fulani mobility, survival and identity in Ghana* (New Brunswick: Transaction Publishers, 2002)

David Foster Wallace interview with *ZDF* in 2003. Excerpt from the interview in which Wallace discusses consumerism here: https://www.youtube.com/watch?v=P1PC1sArw70

David Lipsky, *Although of course you end up becoming yourself: a roadtrip with David Foster Wallace* (New York: Broadway Books, 2010), 39, 84–6

James Olds (1958), 'Self-Stimulation of the Brain', *Science*, 127, 3294

James Olds and Peter Milner (1954), 'Positive reinforcement produced by electrical stimulation of septal area and other regions of rat brain', *Journal of Comparative and Physiological Psychology*, 47(6), 419–427

James Olds (1956), 'Pleasure centers in the brain', *Scientific American*, 195:105–16

Otniel Dror (2016), 'Cold War "Super-Pleasure": Insatiability, Self-stimulation, and the Postwar Brain', *Osiris*, 31(1):227–249

Barry Schwartz, *Paradox of Choice* (New York: HarperCollins, 2004), 10, 104

Barry Schwartz (2005), 'The Paradox of Choice', *TED*, https://www.ted.com/talks/barry_schwartz_on_the_paradox_of_choice?language=en

Xavier Carteret (2012), 'Michel Adanson in Senegal (1749–
1754): A Great Naturalistic and Anthropological Journey
of the Enlightenment', in *Revue d'histoire des sciences*,
65–1 https://www.cairn-int.info/article-E_RHS_651_0005–
michel-adanson-in-senegal-1749–1754.htm

Duane Isely, *One Hundred and One Botanists* (Ames: Iowa
State University Press, 1994), 97–9

Wagieh EL-Saadaw, Said G Youssef and Marwah M Kamal-
EL-Din (2004), 'Fossil palm woods of Egypt: II. Seven
Tertiary Palmoxylon species new to the country', *Review
of Palaeobotany and Palynology*, 129(4), 199–211

Mindy Weisberger (20 November 2015), 'Fossilized Tropical Forest Found in Arctic Norway', *Live Science*, https://
www.livescience.com/52868-fossil-forests-norway.html

Paul Heinrich (2002), 'Louisiana Petrified Wood' http://
www.intersurf.com/~chalcedony/Petwood.html

'Petrified Palmwood', https://statesymbolsusa.org/symbol-
official-item/louisiana/state-dinosaur-fossil/petrified-
palmwood

Alain Rival and Patrice Levang, *Palms of controversies: Oil
palm and development challenges* (Bogor Barat: Centre
for Forestry Research, 2014)

Gerald Wickens, in collaboration with Pat Lowe, *The Baobabs: Pachycauls of Africa, Madagascar and Australia*
(New York: Springer, 2008), 6–10, 331

John Hunwick, *Timbuktu and the Songhay Empire: Al-
Sa'di's Ta'rīkh Al-Sūdān Down to 1613 and other Contemporary Documents* (Boston: Brill, 2003), lvi

Eric Ross, 'A Historical Geography of the Trans-Saharan
Trade', in Graziano Krätli and Ghislaine Lydon, eds., *The
Trans-Saharan Book Trade* (Leiden: Koninklijke Brill,
2011), 1–34

Ivor Wilks (1965), 'A Note on the early spread of Islam in Dagomba', *Transactions of the Historical Society of Ghana*, 8, 87–98

James Fernandez, *Bwiti, An Ethnography of the Religious Imagination in Africa* (Princeton: Princeton University Press, 1982), 470–492

Christian La Fougère et al. (2010), 'Real versus imagined locomotion: a [18F]-FDG PET-fMRI comparison', *Neuroimage*, (50)4, 1589–98

Shane O'Mara, *In Praise of Walking* (London: The Bodley Head, 2019), 63

Richard Byrd, *Alone* (Washington: Island Press, 1938), 10, 99, 118–19, 148, 165, 297

Mihaly Csikszentmihalyi, *Flow: The Psychology of Optimal Experience* (New York: Harper and Row, 1990), 4, 54, 91

Alexandra Starr (7 March 2011), 'What Makes Us Happy? A professor explores our capacity for deep enjoyment and mental well-being', *AARP*, https://www.aarp.org/personal-growth/life-long-learning/info-02–2009/Innovator-Mihaly-Csikszentmihalyi.html

Mihaly Csikszentmihalyi (2004), 'Flow, the Secret to Happiness', *TED*, https://www.ted.com/talks/mihaly_csikszentmihalyi_on_flow/transcript?language=en

Mihaly Csikszentmihalyi, *Finding Flow: the Psychology of Engagement with Everyday Life* (New York: Basic Books, 1997), 111–13

Christopher Burney, *Solitary Confinement* (London: Clerke and Cockeran, 1952)

David Smith (1991), 'Walking as Spiritual Discipline: Henry Thoreau and the Inward Journey', *Soundings: An Interdisciplinary Journal*, 74(1/2), 129–40

Henry David Thoreau, *A Writer's Journal*, ed. Laurence Stapleton (New York: Dover Publications 1960, first published 1851), 64, 176

Henry David Thoreau, 'Walking', in *The Portable Thoreau*, ed. Carl Bode (New York: Viking Press, 1947), 613

Sue Prideaux, *I Am Dynamite! A Life of Nietzsche* (London: Faber & Faber, 2018)

Friedrich Nietzsche, *Ecce Homo: How To Become What You Are*, trans. Duncan Large (Oxford: Oxford University Press, 2007), 21

Ron Chepesiuk (2009), 'Missing the Dark: Health Effects of Light Pollution', *Environmental Health Perspectives*, 117(1): A20–A27

Kimberley Whitehead and Matthew Beaumont (2018), 'The Art of Medicine: Insomnia: A brief cultural history', *The Lancet*, 391(10138): 2408–2409

Gandhi Yetish et al. (2015), 'Natural sleep and its seasonal variations in three pre-industrial societies', *Current Biology*, 25(21): 2862–2868

Kenneth P. Wright et al. (2013), 'Entrainment of the Human Circadian Clock to the Natural Light-Dark Cycle', *Current Biology*, 23(16): 1554–1558

Karen Palmer, *Spellbound: Inside West Africa's Witch Camps* (New York: Free Press, 2010), 49–53

'Reel Women: Episode 1: The Witches of Gambaga (interview with Yaba Badoe)', *Soas Radio*, (29 June 2012), https://soasradio.org/speech/episodes/reel-women-episode-1-witches-gambaga-interview-yaba-badoe

'2013 Country Reports on Human Rights Practices: Ghana', *US Department of State* (27 February 2014), https://www.state.gov/j/drl/rls/hrrpt/2013/af/220119.htm

'Tenzug – Tallensi Settlements', *UNESCO: Tentative Lists* https://whc.unesco.org/en/tentativelists/1392/

Jean Allman and John Parker, *Tongnaab: The History of a West African God* (Bloomington: Indiana University Press, 2005)

Jack Kerouac, *The Dharma Bums* (New York: the Viking Press, 1958), 132

Timothy Wilson et al. (2014), 'Just think: The challenges of the disengaged mind', *Science*, 345(6192): 75–77

Edward Murrow, 'Wire and Lights in a Box', speech given to the convention of the *Radio Television Digital News Association* (15 October 1958), https://rtdna.org/content/edward_r_murrow_s_1958_wires_lights_in_a_box_speech

Chunwang Li et al. (2011), 'Do Père David's Deer Lose Memories of Their Ancestral Predators?', *PLOS One*, 6(8)

Brian Dias and Kerry Ressler (2014), 'Parental olfactory experience influences behavior and neural structure in subsequent generations', *Nature Neuroscience*, 17, 89–96

## Mountains

Lamin Sanneh, *West African Christianity: The Religious Impact* (London: C. Hurst & Co. 1983), chapter 2

Gwendolyn Midlo Hall, *Slavery and African Ethnicities in the Americas* (Chapel Hill: University of North Carolina Press, 2007), 78

Robin Law, *Ouidah: The Social History of a West African Slaving 'Port' 1727–1892* (Oxford: James Currey, 2004), 141, 153

Dennis Laumann (2003), 'A Historiography of German Togoland, or the rise and fall of a "model colony"', *History in Africa*, 30, 195–211

Silke Strickrodt (2001), 'A Neglected Source for the History of Little Popo: The Thomas Miles Papers ca. 1789–1796', *History in Africa*, 28, 293–330

Michael Friedewald, 'Funkentelegrafie und deutsche Kolo-
nien: Technik als Mittel imperialistischer Politik' (ISI,
2001), 61 http://www.friedewald-family.de/Publikationen/
GAGFriedewald.pdf

Timothy Stapleton, *Africa: War and Conflict in the Twentieth Century* (London: Routledge, 2018)

'Togo: Olympio Assassinated' *Facts On File World News
Digest* 16 January 1963, http://www.2facts.com

David Brown (1980), 'Borderline Politics in Ghana: The
National Liberation Movement of Western Togoland',
*The Journal of Modern African Studies*, 18(4), 575–609

Stephen Ellis (1993), 'Rumour and Power in Togo', *Africa:
Journal of the International African Institute*, 63(4),
462–76

Kaye Whiteman (7 February 2005), 'Gnassingbe Eyadema',
*The Guardian*, https://www.theguardian.com/news/2005/
feb/07/guardianobituaries

Douglas Farah (7 September 2001), 'In Togo, the Big Man
Looms Large', *The Washington Post*,
https://www.washingtonpost.com/archive/poli-
tics/2001/09/07/in-togo-the-big-man-looms-
large/1761a072-5636-422f-9b66-28f9751dd6be/?utm_
term=.ef38223f1c0c

Robert LaGamma (10 May 2005), 'Why Togo Matters', *The
New York Times*, https://www.nytimes.com/2005/05/10/
opinion/why-togo-matters.html

'Togo: will history repeat itself?', *Amnesty International*,
20 July 2005, https://www.amnesty.org/download/Docu-
ments/80000/afr570122005en.pdf

John Harrington (29 November 2018), 'From the Solomon
Islands to Liberia: These are the 25 poorest countries in the
world', *USA Today*, https://eu.usatoday.com/story/money/
2018/11/29/poorest-countries-world-2018/38429473/

'Histoire du Togo: Il était une fois Eyadema' https://www. bookgallery.co.il/content/bookpics/129710/frontcover.jpg

Chinua Achebe, *Anthills of the Savannah* (Oxford: Heinemann Educational Publishers, 1987), 128

Eleanor Wachtel, *More Writers & Company* (Toronto: Vintage Canada, 1997) 115–16

Marco Meola, Anna Lazzaro and Josef Zeyer (2015), 'Bacterial Composition and Survival on Sahara Dust Particles Transported to the European Alps', *Frontiers in Microbiology*, https://www.frontiersin.org/articles/10.3389/fmicb.2015.01454/full

M. Arago (1836), 'Arago on Comets', *North American Review*, 42, 196–216

Ellen Gray (22 February 2015), 'NASA Satellite Reveals How Much Saharan Dust Feeds Amazon's Plants', *NASA. gov*, https://www.nasa.gov/content/goddard/nasa-satellite-reveals-how-much-saharan-dust-feeds-amazon-s-plants

Hongbin Yu et al. (2015), 'The fertilizing role of African dust in the Amazon rainforest: A first multiyear assessment based on data from Cloud⊠Aerosol Lidar and Infrared Pathfinder Satellite Observations', *Geophysical Research Letters*, 42(6), 1984–1991
https://agupubs.onlinelibrary.wiley.com/doi/full/10.1002/2015GL063040

'Tassili n'Ajjer', *Unesco*, https://whc.unesco.org/en/list/179/

Marion Perminger, *The Sands of Tamanrasset: the story of Charles de Foucauld* (New York: Hawthorn, 1961)

Paul Lewis (12 July 1981), 'A pilgrimage to a mystic's hermitage in Algeria', *New York Times*

Benoît Hopquin (19 June 2009), 'Essais nucléaires, les irradiés d'In-Ekker', *Le Monde Magazine*, https://www.lemonde.fr/societe/article/2009/06/19/essais-nucleaires-les-irradies-d-in-ekker_1209119_3224.html

'Radiological Conditions at the Former French Nuclear Test Sites in Algeria: Preliminary Assessment and Recommendations', *International Atomic Energy Agency* (Vienna, 2005) https://www-pub.iaea.org/MTCD/publications/PDF/Pub 1215_web_new.pdf

Louis Liebenberg (2006), 'Persistence Hunting by Modern Hunter⊠Gatherers', *Current Anthropology*, 47:6, pp. 1017–26

Richard Lee, 'Population growth and the beginnings of sedentary life among the !Kung Bushmen', in Brian Spooner, ed., *Population growth: Anthropological implications* (Cambridge: MIT Press, 1972), pp. 329–342

Vincent Priessnitz, *The Cold Water Cure: its Principles, Theory and Practice* (London: William Strange, 1843)

Richard Claridge, *Hydropathy; or Cold Water Cure as Practiced by Vincent Priessnitz* (London: James Madden & Co., 1842), 15, 36–39, 50, 56, 71, 83–84

Sebastian Kneipp, *My Water Cure* (Kempton: Jos Koesel, 1886), 3, 327

Nan Shepherd, *The Living Mountain* (Aberdeen: Aberdeen University Press, 1977), 104, 108

Malidoma Somé, *Ritual: Power, Healing and Community* (Columbus: Swan Raven & Company, 1993), 22

Olaudah Equiano, *The Interesting Narrative and Other Writings*, ed. Vincent Carretta (London: Penguin Books, 1995, first published 1789), xxix, 32–9, 46–8, 52–9, 66–7, 174, 104

Dean Falk, *The Fossil Chronicles: how two controversial discoveries changed our view of human evolution* (Berkeley: University of California Press, 2011)

Sue Armstrong (9 September 1995), 'Taung Child "fell from the sky"', *New Scientist*

Brian Regal, *Human evolution: a guide to the debates* (Santa Barbara: Abc-Clio, 2004)

Keith Stewart Thomson (1991), 'Piltdown Man: The Great English Mystery Story', *American Scientist*

Erin Wayman (6 August 2012), 'Becoming Human: The Evolution of Walking Upright', *Smithsonian Magazine*, https://www.smithsonianmag.com/science-nature/becoming-human-the-evolution-of-walking-upright-13837658/

Kate Bartlett (17 February 2011), 'Piltdown Man: Britain's Greatest Hoax', *BBC History*, https://www.bbc.co.uk/history/ancient/archaeology/piltdown_man_01.shtml

Ryszard, Kapuściński, *The Soccer War*, trans. by William Brand (London: Granta, 1990), 123, 11

Harris Lentz, *Heads of State and Governments since 1945* (London: Routledge, 1994), 89–90

Patrick Claffey, 'Kérékou the Chameleon, Master of Myth', in Julia Strauss and Donal Cruise O'Brien, eds., *Staging Politics: Power and Performance in Asia and Africa* (London: IB Taurus, 2007), 99

'Après 29 ans de pouvoir, le Président Kérékou tire sa révérence' (6 April 2006), *The New Humanitarian* http://www.thenewhumanitarian.org/fr/actualit%C3%A9s/2006/04/06/apr%C3%A8s-29-ans-de-pouvoir-le-pr%C3%A9sident-k%C3%A9r%C3%A9kou-tire-sa-r%C3%A9v%C3%A9rence

Femke van Zeijl (12 November 2016), 'The Oba of Benin Kingdom: A history of the monarchy', *Al Jazeera Arts & Culture*, https://www.aljazeera.com/indepth/features/2016/10/oba-benin-kingdom-history-monarchy-161031161559752.html

J. Cameron Monroe (2007), 'Continuity, Revolution or Evolution on the Slave Coast of West Africa? Royal Architecture and Political Order in Precolonial Dahomey', *The Journal of African History*, 48(3)

Robin Law (1989), 'Slave-Raiders and Middlemen, Monopolists and Free-Traders: The Supply of Slaves for the Atlantic Trade in Dahomey c. 1715–1850', *The Journal of African History*, 30(1), p. 46

Robin Law (1997), 'The Politics of Commercial Transition: Factional Conflict in Dahomey in the Context of the Ending of the Atlantic Slave Trade', *Journal of African History*, 38: 213–33, 229

Erika Kraus and Felicie Reid, *Benin* (Other Places Publishing 2010), 16

Jim Haskins, *Black Stars: African Heroes* (Hoboken: John Wiley & Sons, 2005), 55–9

Douglas Falen, *African Science: Witchcraft, Vodun and Healing in Southern Benin* (Madison: University of Wisconsin Press, 2018), 99

Tony Naden (1996), Ancestor Non-worship in Mampruli, *Lexikos* 6:71–103, http://lexikos.journals.ac.za/pub/article/viewFile/1026/542

Mahommah Gardo Baquaqua and Samuel Moore, *Biography of Mahommah G. Baquaqua, a Native of Zoogoo, in the Interior of Africa* (Detroit: Geo. E. Pomeroy & Co., 1854)

Ralph Waldo Emerson, 'Goethe; or, the writer', in *Essays & Lectures* (New York: Literary Classics of the United States, 1983, first published 1850), 746

John Wilford (15 August 1997), 'Human's Earliest Footprints Discovered', *New York Times*

David Keys (7 February 2014), 'Meet the million-year-olds: Human footprints found in Britain are the oldest ever seen outside of Africa, *Independent*

Matthew Moore (7 July 2010), 'Norfolk earliest known settlement in northern Europe', *The Telegraph*

'Gaddafi: Africa's "king of kings"', *BBC News*, 29 August 2008, http://news.bbc.co.uk/1/hi/world/africa/7588033.stm

Joan Wescott (1962), 'The Sculpture and Myths of Eshu-Elegba, the Yoruba Trickster. Definition and Interpretation in Yoruba Iconography', *Africa: Journal of the International African Institute*, 32(4): 336–354

Maya Deren, *Divine Horsemen: The Living Gods of Haiti* (London: Thames and Hudson, 1953), 114–116, 60–61

Laurent Dubois, *Haiti: The Aftershocks of History* (New York: Picador, 2012), 19, 21

Steeve Coupeau, *The History of Haiti* (Westport: Greenwood Press, 2008), 15

Molefi Kete Asante and Ama Mazama (eds), *Encyclopedia of African Religion, Volume 1* (Los Angeles: Sage, 2009), 131

Laurent Dubois, *Avengers of the New World: The Story of the Haitian Revolution* (Cambridge, The Belknap Press of Harvard University Press: 2004), 7

Jack Richard Censer and Lynn Avery Hunt, *Liberty, Equality, Fraternity Exploring the French Revolution* (University Park: Penn State University Press, 2001), 124

Deborah Jenson (2012), 'Jean-Jacques Dessalines and the African Character of the Haitian Revolution', *The William and Mary Quarterly*, 69(3)

'Pat Robertson says Haiti paying for "pact to the devil"', *CNN*, 13 January 2010, http://edition.cnn.com/2010/US/01/13/haiti.pat.robertson/index.html

Samuel Otero and Toyin Falola, *Yemoja: Gender, Sexuality, and Creativity in the Latina/o and Afro-Atlantic Diasporas* (Albany: State University of New York Press, 2013), xvii–xxiv

John Berryman, *The Dream Songs* (New York: Farrar, Strauss & Giroux, 1969), Dream Song #153 (page 172), Dream Song #235 (page 255)

'El Santuario de Chimayo, New Mexico', *National Park Service*, https://www.nps.gov/nr/travel/american_latino_heritage/El_Santuario_de_Chimayo.html

Kazuaki Tanahashi, 'Fundamentals of Dogen's Thoughts', *Tricycle*, February 2009, https://tricycle.org/trikedaily/fundamentals-of-dogens-thoughts/

Carl Jung, *Memories, Dreams, Reflections*, ed. by Aniela Jaffé, trans. by Richard and Clara Winston (New York: Random House, 1961), 226, 247–251

Meredith Sabini, *The Earth has a Soul: CG Jung on Nature, Technology & Modern Life* (Berkeley: North Atlantic Books, 2002), 30–31, 35–37, 68–69

Claire Dunne, *Carl Jung: Wounded Healer of the Soul: An Illustrated Biography* (New York: Watkins, 2015), 71

Gerhard Wehr, *Jung: A Biography*, trans. by D.M. Weeks (Boulder: Shambhala, 1987), 225

## Sea

Alex van Stipriaan, 'Watramama / Mami Wata: Three Centuries of Creolization of a Water Spirit in West Africa, Suriname and Europe', in Gordon Collier and Ulrich Fleischmann, eds., *A Pepper-Pot of Cultures: Aspect of Creolization in the Caribbean* (Amsterdam: Editions Rodophi, 2003), 323–32

Henry John Drewal (1988), 'Interpretation, Invention, and Re-Presentation in the Worship of Mami Wata', *Journal of Folklore Research*, 25(1/2), 101–139

Henry John Drewal (1988), 'Mermaids, Mirrors, and Snake Charmers: Igbo Mami Wata Shrines', *African Arts*, 21(2), 38–45

Mama Zogbé, *Mami Wata: Africa's Ancient Goddess Unveiled* (Martinez: Mami Wata Healers Society of North America, 2007)